MY MONEY AND ME

WE'RE TALKING NOW

Books by the Author:

Gathering (first novel in series)
Drifting (second novel in series)
Overcoming (third novel in series)
The Pet Therapist (novel)
AI Guidance to Masculine Harmony (self help)

Balancing Masculinity. (therapeutics tales)

MY MONEY AND ME

WE'RE TALKING NOW

A psychological guide to reclaiming your finances and self-respect

Henrik Kruse

Contents

Intro: A Little About Money — and a Lot About People....................vii

Chapter 1 Mental Accounting....................1
Chapter 2 The Budget That Lies....................7
Chapter 3 The Conscious Choice....................17
Chapter 4 The Different Rooms of Money....................21
Chapter 5 When Money Works in the Dark....................27
Chapter 6 Feeling Rich, Regardless of Income....................35
Chapter 7 Finances as a Life Decision....................51
Chapter 8 On True and False Security....................61
Chapter 9 Money and Personality....................79
Chapter 10 When Dreams Become Domains....................87
Chapter 11 Quality or Quantity?....................111
Chapter 12 Inheritance, Gifts, and the Sacred Money....................121
Chapter 13 When Finances Have Collapsed....................137
Chapter 14 When Love and Money Meet....................143
Chapter 15 The Economic Ecosystem....................161

A Personal Afterword....................181
Appendix: The People Behind the Ideas....................183

Intro

A LITTLE ABOUT MONEY — AND A LOT ABOUT PEOPLE

I had never written about money before. And maybe that's exactly why I ended up doing it.

Because this is not a traditional finance book. You won't find investment advice, budgeting templates, or savings strategies in the pages ahead. What you will find are questions. Stories. Moods. And maybe a moment of recognition that helps you see your money in a new light.

When I began writing, I had no plan. Just a feeling: that money means more than we think—just not necessarily in the ways we're used to.

Throughout my working life, I've gathered some experiences that stuck with me. In a large organization where I was one of many department heads, we all worked with nearly identical financial conditions. And yet, the outcomes we created were strikingly different. Some barely managed to keep things afloat—while others, somehow, pulled off major projects and achieved far more than the budget should have allowed. The same financial framework—in different hands—produced wildly different possibilities.

That left an impression on me. And it echoed something I had already noticed among my friends: how some people always seem to struggle financially, while others always manage to stay on top—even though their incomes are more or less the same.

As my interest in money deepened, I started digging further. I became curious about ideas like mental accounting, circular finances, and a more ecological approach to finances. I discovered that there is, in fact, a more holistic—even human—way of thinking about money and its role in our lives. And that sparked something in me.

Yes, finances are about money. But just as much about the people managing it. And when you look a little closer, it becomes clear that behavior and psychology play a central role.

That realization became the driving force behind this book.

The Four Voices in the Back of My Mind

As I wrote, I realized I wasn't alone. Among many, four voices in particular inspired me. Each, in their own field, had made discoveries that resonated deeply.

The first voice belonged to **Brené Brown**.

She reminded me that many of us carry shame about not having our finances under control.

Shame about not being able to save, to pay back debt, to invest wisely.

Shame about feeling poor—even when it doesn't seem rational.

She said that vulnerability is courage.

And I came to see that just looking our finances in the eye—without making excuses—takes *courage.*

The second voice was **Morgan Housel**.

He wrote that money isn't about math—it's about psychology.

He helped me realize that I—and maybe you, too—often act with money based on emotions, stories, hopes, and habits.

Not because we're foolish, but because we're human.

He opened my eyes to this insight:

"My finances are not just a spreadsheet—they're a story about me."

The third voice was **Vicki Robin**.

She asked: "What are you trading your life for?"

That hit home.

She reminded me that money isn't just a medium of exchange—it's life energy. Time. Freedom.

And that if we're not careful, we may end up trading away what truly matters for things we don't actually need.

She showed me that financial awareness isn't about restriction or limitation—it's about possibility.

And then there was **Kate Northrup**.

She said:

"Your relationship with money reflects your relationship with yourself."

She spoke of self-worth. Of what you might call 'loving accountability.'

Not with harshness and spreadsheets—but with gentleness and clarity.

She asked what we allow ourselves. And whether we even believe we have the right to feel financially safe—even if we don't get everything 'right.'

These four voices didn't write this book. But they helped set the tone and the mood.

Maybe they'll form a backdrop—alongside my own experiences and your reflections—for the journey you're about to begin.

At the end of the book, you'll find an appendix with brief profiles of these four thought leaders, along with six others I'll refer to later.

What Can You Get Out of Reading This Book?

You'll get new words and images for how you relate to money.

You'll discover that money isn't just about numbers and spreadsheets—but about feelings, habits, and personal stories.

You'll learn to see your finances as something connected to your history, your values, and your everyday life.

You'll begin to understand why you do what you do—and how you can begin to change it.

You'll gain insight into the psychological and emotional forces that shape your financial decisions—often without you realizing it.

And you'll get tools to change those patterns. Not by forcing yourself, but by understanding yourself.

You'll feel less alone—and maybe even richer than you thought.

Through examples, short stories, and personal reflection, you'll start to recognize yourself.

And maybe you'll discover that you already have more freedom, more resources, and more value in your life than you previously saw.

How the Book Is Structured

The book begins with shorter chapters, gradually becoming longer as we go deeper.

Each chapter contains:

- A scene or situation you might recognize in yourself
- A thought or theory that puts it into perspective
- A small question or exercise you can take with you

You can read the book cover to cover—or flip to the chapter that speaks to where you are in your life right now.

You're Not Alone

To make it more relatable, I've chosen to let two characters follow us through the book: Maria and Jonas.

They aren't real—but they're not entirely fictional either.

They're a composite of things I've heard, seen, and experienced when it comes to money.

Maria lives in the suburbs, has a job and a family, but feels stuck.

She's done everything 'right'—and still feels financially inadequate.

Jonas lives in the city, lives simply, has opted out of the traditional career and financial path—he feels free, but also alone, and sometimes unsure whether he's being responsible enough.

The two don't meet until the very end of the book, at a lecture that gathers and reflects on the book's main insights.

Until then, we follow them separately, getting a glimpse into their different habits and reflections.

They're meant as a guide—to make the themes we explore feel more human and easier to relate to.

Chapter 1

MENTAL ACCOUNTING

Why finances aren't just about numbers—but about meaning

Money isn't just money. On a psychological level, it holds very different values for us. That's a relative truth I was already puzzled by as a child. A birthday gift of $20 that I could use on anything felt way more exciting than $40 earmarked for clothes.

I call it a relative truth because it's both true and false—depending on your point of view. A hundred dollars is a hundred dollars, no matter what I buy. And from a broad and objective perspective, it's also true and clear: If I considered all of myself, I needed both pocket money and clothes.

But it was also true that I appreciated the pocket money more. I felt freedom and joy attached to it—whereas the clothing money felt like something necessary, a bit boring, and imposed.

That same duality shows up in adulthood. We'll spend $100 on dinner without blinking—but think $10 for parking is outrageous. When you look closer, it's not really about the amount. It's about context and emotion.

Jonas

Jonas was staring at his online banking. $340. It wasn't catastrophic—but he still felt poor.

He had just received $1000 for a small freelance project and had imagined it would give him some breathing room. Now the money was nearly gone: some groceries, some electricity, the dentist bill. And the feeling of freedom had nearly vanished.

He stared at the numbers. They looked 'okay,' really. But they didn't feel good.

Later that day, he went out to eat with a friend. They had pizza and beer and shared a dessert. It cost $60. Jonas had no problem paying the bill. "It's social. That's important."

Same money—two completely different feelings.

Money has domains—and meaning

Psychologists call it mental accounting. Behind the slightly technical term is a key observation: We organize our finances into internal compartments or 'boxes.' One for food. One for fun. One for vacations. One for debt. One for dreams.

The interesting part is that money changes psychological value depending on which box it sits in.

We think and feel differently about money we 'must' use—and money we're 'allowed' to use. Some money feels like freedom. Other money feels like obligation. We may feel guilty using some accounts—and relieved using others. We have 'household money,' 'hidden money,' 'shared money,' 'my own money,' 'inheritance money,' 'emergency money.'

It's not rational. But it's deeply human. And it varies from person to person—and from situation to situation.

Where does the idea come from?

The concept of *mental accounting* was developed by American behavioral economist **Richard H. Thaler**. He received the Nobel Prize in Economics in 2017—not for a classic economic formula, but for his groundbreaking insights into how people actually behave around money.

Thaler was one of the first to insist on bringing psychology into economics. He showed that we don't just see money as one lump sum. We divide it into mental accounts, each with its own emotional and symbolic logic.

And this is the core of his theory: We make financial decisions differently depending on which 'account' the money belongs to in our internal bookkeeping. A tax payment feels more painful than an automatic transfer, even if the amount is the same. We spend gift money more easily than savings. We're more likely to keep gambling in a casino if we're playing with 'winnings' than with what's in our wallet.

Thaler also showed that these accounts don't necessarily follow logical or objective criteria. They're influenced by feelings, stories, and social norms. A vacation fund becomes almost *sacred*. A debt fund becomes *unpleasant*. An emergency fund often sits *empty*—even when there's money elsewhere.

Thaler's point wasn't that we should behave more rationally. Quite the opposite. He believed we need to understand how we actually think and act. And from there, we can start making better choices—not perfect ones, but more *conscious* ones.

His research isn't just a theory about money—it's a theory about us. About how we handle complexity, responsibility, and emotion in something as seemingly neutral as finances. And that's exactly why mental accounting is such a powerful tool for self-understanding.

Maria

Maria had made an envelope labeled 'kids allowance.' She liked systems—and it felt safe knowing the money was right there, marked and set aside.

But when her car needed repairs, she borrowed from the envelope—'just until Friday.'

She didn't think much of it until a week later when it was time to hand out the allowance. Then she felt a little uneasy. Not because of the money itself. But because she had broken a promise. Not to her children—but to herself.

She knew it wasn't just about finances. It was something moral. Something about the kind of person—and mother—she wanted to be.

Small everyday examples

Ali feels financially irresponsible because he doesn't have savings—but he pays his sister's phone bill and sends money to his mother every month.

Louise feels like a 'loser' because she can't afford a new car—but she's just paid down her debt and has three well-deserved weeks of vacation ahead.

What they have in common is that they measure their financial situation by an internal standard that doesn't always match reality. It's not about what they have—but how they *view* what they have.

We're not all the same—and that's the whole point

Our relationship with money isn't just about the numbers. It depends on how we're wired inside.

Some grew up with lack. Others with plenty. Some learned to talk openly about money. Others learned to stay silent.

Some feel free when they spend. Others feel free when they save.

That's why two people with the exact same income can feel entirely different—one rich, the other poor.

That's why this book doesn't start with a budget. It starts with a look inward.

Inner organization—a psychological ecology

When we talk later in the book about 'ecological finances,' we don't mean the environment or climate. We're talking about internal coherence—a kind of psychological balance, where finances aren't isolated, but integrated into the rest of life.

Everything in us is connected: our feelings, experiences, habits, and values. And our finances are part of that system. They shape:

- How we see ourselves
- What we believe we're entitled to
- What we think others think of us
- How we react when things go wrong

That's why it makes sense to understand finances not just as something external—but as something internal too.

Exercise: The Meaning of Your Money

Make a list or drawing of your financial boxes.
What do you call them?
Which money feels easy to spend—and which feels wrong?
Which money feels 'safe'?
Which money feels like obligation, guilt, freedom, love?
Look at your list. Consider what your answers say about you.
Not to judge—but to understand.

Chapter 2

THE BUDGET THAT LIES

Why We Try to Control Ourselves—
And What We Overlook

When We Try to Control Ourselves with Numbers

Maria sat across from the bank advisor. He let his pen glide down a printed sheet with green and red fields.

"If we're going to consider a loan," he said kindly, "then it's important that we put together a realistic budget."

Maria nodded. She felt like she should have done it long ago.

"So you have about $300 left after fixed expenses?" he asked.

"Yes… or… well… if nothing unexpected comes up."

She smiled awkwardly and felt a tightness in her stomach.

This wasn't just a form. It was a judgment. An evaluation.

And at the core: an attempt to gain control over something within herself that she had never truly managed.

Jonas had felt the same way the year before. He had made his own Excel sheet—color-coded and well thought out.

His hope was that the budget would make him better: more adult, more responsible, more in control.

But paradoxically, it didn't work. The longer he tried to stick to it, the more incompetent he felt.

In reality, he had created a spreadsheet policeman—judging him every time he was just being himself.

I think many people feel this way about budgets:

They don't offer real support and often end up as expectations we can't fulfill. They don't necessarily reflect reality—but rather an ideal that highlights the gap between the life we live and the life we believe we're supposed to live.

From that perspective, the budget isn't a kind helper—but a form of self-discipline in disguise.

We create it to gain control, but we end up using it to fight parts of ourselves we don't yet understand or haven't embraced.

The budget becomes a tool for self-manipulation.

We hope that if we just follow it, we'll become the person we want to be.

But that rarely works—because we start in the wrong place.

A Bit Like a Diet

It's like classic New Year's resolutions:

"I'll run every morning."

"I'll only eat sugar on weekends."

The intentions are honest—but often built on self-criticism.

And when we can't stick to the plan, it's not just the goal that suffers—it's us.

It's the same with budgets:

When we fall outside our own systems, the result isn't just financial trouble—but psychological reactions.

Guilt. Shame. Frustration. Self-contempt.

Because we've used the budget to try to control parts of ourselves we've never really faced:

Our impulses. Our needs. Our fears. Our longings.

An Invisible Hierarchy

When we build a budget without knowing ourselves, we risk basing it on values we think are right—but that don't really fit who we are.

We might believe that food 'should' cost a certain amount. That we ought to spend less on clothes. That we should have our retirement sorted. That we can't go on vacation without a safety net.

But who says so? Where do these rules come from?

Maybe childhood. Maybe societal ideals. Maybe shame or fear.

And when we can't live up to them, we don't just feel like the budget isn't working—we feel like we're not working.

When the Spreadsheet Takes Over the Person

In that way, the budget can shift from being a support to becoming an overbearing judge. A piece of paper watching us. An Excel sheet telling us we're not okay.

But it's not the budget's fault.

It's the way we use it that's flawed.

We use it as a psychological tool—but without asking the key question:

"What part of me am I really trying to control—and why?"

Feelings Aren't a Disturbance—They're the Drivers

At one point I realized I used two completely different parts of my brain when I planned my finances and when I lived with them.

Planning happened in the rational part—charts, logic, overview.

But in daily life, it was a different part that took over:

The emotional, vulnerable, and unpredictable one.

That meant I made financial choices that didn't match the plan—not because I was lazy or weak, but because I was human.

Because life is full of feelings:

We get tired. We get tempted. We feel lonely, generous, anxious, stressed, hopeful, joyful.

And all these emotions influence our financial choices.

It becomes a kind of short-circuit:

One part plans, and another part executes—with no mutual understanding.

The Budget Misses the Most Important Thing

It may look smart.

It may be detailed, color-coded, and precisely calculated.

But it misses one crucial factor: *You.*

It doesn't know your emotional patterns.

It doesn't know your relationships.

It doesn't understand that gifts aren't just expenses—they're symbols.

It doesn't understand that a coffee on the go might be your only breathing space of the day.

It doesn't understand that we use money as language: to say sorry, to celebrate, to soothe, to connect.

And that's why budgets often feel unrealistic—Not because they're poorly made, but because they miss the most important element in your finances: *yourself.*

The failure isn't that you can't stick to a budget.

The failure is thinking you *should* be able to.

Example: The Invisible Gift Account

Maria realized after a few months that she almost always went over budget in December and March. Not on food. Not on entertainment. But on gifts.

She had never thought of it as a pattern—but looking back, it dawned on her:

In December, she always wanted to give a little extra.

In March, several family members had birthdays.

And she *wanted* to give gifts—because that was her way of showing love.

It wasn't in her budget.

But it was in her heart.

And so the money went out anyway.

Not as a problem—but as part of her identity.

When the Budget Reveals the Conflict Between Me and My Ideal

Many people realize their budget was actually created by a fictional version of themselves.

A version that never gets tired.

Never gets tempted.

Never needs a break or a celebration.

A version with iron discipline and a predictable emotional life.

But then comes real life.

And every time we deviate from the plan, we feel wrong—without questioning who made the plan in the first place.

A New Thought: *You* Before the Budget

Maybe we need to start somewhere else—not with the question:

"How can I fit my life into this spreadsheet?"

But instead ask:

"What does my life actually look like? What matters to me? What values, dreams, and needs do I have?"

And only then:

"How can my budget reflect that—and help me live the life I want?"

The budget should not be a judge. It should be a mirror.

Not a control system—but a companion. A flexible tool that is revised as your priorities change.

And most importantly: It should make sense to you.

A good budget doesn't begin with control.

It begins with *self-respect.*

There's a big difference between being disciplined and being responsible.

Discipline often means following rules—even when they no longer make sense.

Responsibility means standing by your choices—and adjusting them when life changes.

A human budget doesn't start with restrictions—it starts with questions:

What do I need?

What do I long for?

What do I want to be able to say yes to—and no to?

Honoring Who You Are

When you create a budget that actually fits you, you might experience for the first time that finances aren't just about 'getting things under control'—but about taking yourself seriously.

It's not laziness or irresponsibility to change your budget.

It's maturity.

It's not irresponsible to admit that a plan isn't working.

It's responsible to adjust—so that what you do with your money aligns with the life you want to live.

The Budget as a Psychological Buffer

There's another way to use a budget—not as control, but as support.

Not as a judge, but as a friendly foresight.

One of the most constructive ways to work with a budget is to set aside a fixed amount for *unforeseen expenses*. It may sound contradictory—how can you budget for the unexpected? But that's exactly the point: we *know* there will be expenses we can't precisely plan. We just don't know when—or how big.

It could be anything from car repairs, fines, and dentist bills to unexpected gifts or family emergencies. These kinds of expenses often feel particularly annoying—not just because they cost money, but because they hit us mentally, as *disruptions* to the plan.

But if we've already set money aside for them, the emotional impact changes.

Suddenly, the *unexpected is expected*—and therefore not a crisis, but a part of the system.

For example:

If I get a parking ticket, and I know I've set money aside for such things, I don't have to be upset. The money is ready.

If the car needs repairs and it's expensive, it won't throw off my daily budget.

If I want to give a gift—and I have a gift budget—I can do it without guilt.

In that way, the budget becomes a *psychological buffer.* It softens emotional reactions and helps us remain calm in situations that would otherwise stress us out. It's not control for its own sake—but a way to care for your future self.

From a behavioral economics perspective, this holds an important insight: We make worse decisions when we're under pressure. By preparing for the unforeseen, we avoid the stress that could otherwise lead to poor choices—and at the same time feel more dignified and prepared.

You could call it a *kind budget.* A budget that doesn't restrict life—but makes space for its waves.

The Budget as a Principle-Based Shield

There are also expenses we don't want to debate with ourselves.

In political budgets, people sometimes talk about 'protected areas'—categories that are off-limits, even during cuts. It might be foreign aid, welfare, or green initiatives. The idea is that cutting here undermines your core values.

It can be the same with personal finances.

Some expenses we just *want* to have—no matter what the finances looks like.

It could be support for a cause we believe in.

It could be gifts to someone we'll always be there for.

It could be a religious commitment, a promise to ourselves, or something rooted in deep life experience.

When we designate these expenses as *protected budget items,* we create peace. We remove doubt and shield what matters from the pressures of daily life.

An example might be:

A father who's decided to sponsor a child in the developing world for every child he has himself. It's a decision he'll never question—not even in hard financial times. So he creates a fixed, non-negotiable item in his budget.

That gives him a sense of freedom. Not because he has a lot of money—but because he doesn't have to negotiate his values every month.

In **behavioral economics**, this is about reducing decision fatigue. We know repeated choices and doubts wear us down. By institutionalizing our principles in the budget, we don't just save money—we save energy and preserve integrity.

In this light, the budget isn't a place for self-control—but a place for self-respect.

Exercise: The Budget Portrait

This exercise isn't about fixing anything.

It's about understanding something.

It's not a test—you can't do it wrong.

Just be as honest as you can with yourself.

1. Write Your Honest Budget

Start with your actual spending from the past 14 days.

Not the planned budget. The real one.

Write it down in categories that make sense to you.

For example:

- Food
- Transportation
- Housing
- Experiences

- Gifts
- 'Small things'
- Feelings? (Yes—some expenses are emotional)

2. Look at the Numbers Like a Picture. Imagine Your Spending Tells a Story.

What does this picture say about you?
What do you prioritize—without realizing it?
What do you neglect—even though you think it's important?
What are you maybe ashamed of?
What are you proud of?
What would a kind observer say if they saw this budget?

3. Write a Short Text: 'My Financial Self-Portrait'

Use 5—10 lines to describe how you see yourself financially—based on what you just discovered.

Not how you think you should be. But how you experience yourself.

You might begin with:
"When I look at my real spending, I discover…"
"I think I've tried to be a person who…"
"I'm surprised that…"
"I like that I…"
"I think my next step might be to…"

This exercise isn't the end of something—it's the beginning of something new.

Chapter 3

THE CONSCIOUS CHOICE

From Self-Criticism to Self-Respect

A Choice Made in Secret

Maria had never really thought about the way she worked as a financial decision. She worked part-time. Not because she couldn't find anything else, but because she had chosen it. She loved the flexibility. It allowed her to pick up the kids early, help her mother, and get involved in volunteer work that mattered to her.

And yet she felt ashamed. Because the job didn't offer much financial breathing room. And in a time where success is often measured by paychecks and pensions, her choice felt wrong. As if she had given up. As if she had failed—maybe not others, but herself.

Until one day, in the middle of a conversation with a colleague, she heard herself say:

"It was actually a choice. I chose it. And I would choose it again."

She went quiet for a moment. It felt like a truth that had been waiting to be said aloud. She hadn't taken the easy way. She had taken the meaningful one. And now she could begin to own it.

A Choice Without a Speech

Jonas had taken a different path. He recently started working extra hours on Saturdays at an electronics store. Not because it was his dream job. But because it gave him the breathing space in his budget—and the freedom to stay in his apartment without constant financial pressure.

He didn't tell many people. No one applauded him. No one called him brave or responsible. And maybe that's exactly why he felt something special the first time he received his paycheck: a sense of having *chosen*. Not just reacted, not just survived—but chosen.

There were no fanfares. But there was dignity.

When Money Choices Are Life Choices

We often talk about money as if it's neutral. As if it's just a tool, not a carrier of meaning. But that's not true. Money is loaded with emotions and values. It reflects what we prioritize. Who we try to be. What we dare to hope for—and what we no longer believe we can have.

That's why finances aren't just practical. They're also a language. A set of symbolic actions we use to navigate life.

Imagine if, for a week, you weren't allowed to use words—only money. How would you show love? How would you comfort yourself? How would you say sorry, celebrate something, mark a boundary?

Money isn't just currency. It's emotional communication.

A Jacket With a Message

Jonas bought an expensive jacket on a Monday. He told himself it was necessary—his old one was worn out. But as he held the jacket in his hands, he knew it wasn't just about practical clothing. It was a gift to himself. A quiet protest against a week in which he had felt invisible. The jacket said: "I'm allowed to take up space." It wasn't a bad reason. It was just a reason he hadn't acknowledged.

A Membership—and a Goodbye

Maria canceled her gym membership. The card had hung around for years—a monthly reminder of something she 'should' be doing but never got around to. When she finally canceled it, it didn't feel like a defeat. It felt like honesty. She wasn't saying no to exercise. She was saying yes to being real with herself.

Taking Responsibility—With Awareness

When we start seeing money as *expression*—not just transaction—something shifts within us. We become more aware. We start taking responsibility. Not as duty, but as integrity. A choice to spend less can be a choice for freedom. A choice to spend more can be a choice for joy. A choice to say no can be a choice for self-respect.

Money says something. The question is: *Does it say what you mean?*

Identity and Finances

We rarely talk about money as an identity marker. But often, that's exactly what it is. It tells us—and others—who we're trying to be. Many of us spend money to resemble people we admire. Or to avoid resembling people we've distanced ourselves from. Others spend almost nothing—but still feel guilty for not living up to the image of 'the good life.'

Our finances become a mirror we're constantly trying to polish. A mirror where we look for a version of ourselves we can stand behind.

We often ask ourselves:

"How do I get control of my finances?"

But maybe we should ask more often:

"Who am I trying to be—with my money?"

It's not just about spending. It's about direction. About life choices. And it starts small—in the grocery store, in the calendar, in the quiet choices we make without saying them out loud.

A *no* to something you usually *say* yes to. A yes to something you've always postponed. One conscious choice—that points in your direction.

Chapter 4

THE DIFFERENT ROOMS OF MONEY

How Money Behaves Differently in Life's Many Areas

This chapter is about something we rarely talk about—but all experience: Money doesn't always behave the same. It depends on which area of life it moves through. In some places, it creates security. In others, doubt. And in some situations, it creates tension—not just between people, but within ourselves.

So we'll explore how money behaves differently across life's domains—and what happens when those domains collide. At the end, you'll get the chance to map out your own financial spaces, so you can begin to see where your decisions land—and why they sometimes feel wrong, even when they look right on paper.

The Invisible Spaces of Finance

We often believe that money is neutral—that it works the same everywhere. But that's not true. Across all cultures and eras, people have organized money into different domains: care, exchange, honor, survival, gifts, freedom, obligation.

And each domain has its own rules. You don't give money to your mother with the same feeling as when you pay rent. You don't buy a gift with the same feeling as when you pay a bill. You don't choose clothes the same way when going to a job interview as when picking up your kids.

The same amount can feel completely different depending on the context. Money changes character—and function—depending on where it shows up.

Domain Thinking: A Psychological Map

When we start seeing finances as a landscape of domains, some things become clearer:

- We're not inconsistent—we're context-driven.
- We begin to understand why some money choices feel easy, and others feel wrong.
- We start to see how we (unconsciously) prioritize different areas of life—and where things may be out of balance.

If you often think, "I should be able to make it all work," it might be because your domains are pulling in different directions. The problem isn't you—it's the complexity of the situation.

Four Domains at Play

Home and Family

Maria wanted to create a cozy home. Soft rugs. Good coffee. A warm lamp in the corner. But every time she bought something, a voice popped up: "Is this necessary? Shouldn't that money have been used more wisely?"

At home, money quickly becomes symbolic. It can signal care—"I'm taking care of you." But it can also raise doubts—"Is this appreciated?" "Am I giving too much?" "Am I doing it for them—or for myself?"

Home is often the most emotionally charged domain. Here, finances rarely concern consumption alone—but love, responsibility, and the longing to do what's right.

Work and Achievement

Jonas got a small raise. He should have been happy. But the feeling never came. He was working more. More stressed. And the money disappeared again—into transport, food, necessities. It didn't feel like success.

At work, money often becomes a marker of identity. "Am I worth something?" "Have I made it?" "Do others see me as someone who has it together?"

Here, we don't just measure results—we measure ourselves. And it's rarely fair.

Leisure and Social Relationships

A group of friends goes out to eat regularly. Everything seems relaxed—on the surface. But one of them can't really afford it. She doesn't say anything but picks the cheapest item on the menu and avoids eye contact when the bill arrives.

In this domain, money becomes a mask. We want to fit in. We want to belong. So we don't say we're financially stretched. Instead, we pay a price to stay included—often both financially and emotionally.

Body and Health

Jonas bought a heart rate monitor. Maria canceled her gym membership. Both choices were about the body—but also about self-image and responsibility.

"Am I doing this for myself—or to meet expectations?"

"Is this self-care—or control?"

Health is a domain where money quickly becomes value-laden. Guilt and pride sit side by side. We want to do the right thing. But what is the right thing—for you?

When Domains Collide

It's rarely possible to satisfy all domains at once.

Maria wanted to take fewer shifts and help her mother more during the week. But the numbers didn't add up. She felt like she was failing—as a daughter, mother, and colleague.

When life's domains pull in different directions, friction arises:

- You spend money on your children—and lose the chance to save.
- You choose health—but say no to social things.
- You work more—and see less of those you love.
- You secure your finances—but feel trapped.

These clashes aren't signs that you're choosing wrong. They're signs that life is complex—and that your choices have consequences across domains.

The Invisible Hierarchy

Some domains win. Others get neglected. We often only notice when something feels empty:

When the body says stop. When relationships fade. When we wake up and feel, "This isn't me."

Domain thinking lets you see your life as a map—and your money as movements between fields.

The question isn't whether you have 'control of your finances.'

The question is: Do you have a conscious relationship with where your money goes—and what it means to you?

Exercise: Map Your Financial Spaces

Draw a circle and divide it like a pie chart. Name the sections after your life areas:

For example: work, family, health, leisure, housing, relationships, personal growth, etc.

In each slice: Write down some of your expenses in that area.

What do you spend money on? What would you like to spend more—or less—on?

Ask yourself:

- Which areas take up the most space?
- Is that intentional?
- Is there something you miss prioritizing?

Write down one thing you'd like to adjust.

Not to 'get it all under control,' but to make things more aligned.

You'll begin to understand how your money moves—and which spaces you want to make more room for.

Chapter 5

WHEN MONEY WORKS IN THE DARK

On Self-Deception, Avoidance, and Financial Shadow Behavior

Where Does the Money Go—And Why Don't We Dare Look at It?

This chapter is not here to judge you.

It's here to help you see something you may have started turning away from.

Most people have a corner of their finances they'd rather not look at. A bank statement that's never opened. A habit they won't admit. A decision they know wasn't great—but that they've repeated anyway.

And that's human.

We avoid what makes us feel ashamed. We numb what hurts.

We lie a little—not to others, but to ourselves.

That doesn't mean we're irresponsible.

It once again shows that money isn't just about numbers—it's about story, self-image, and vulnerability.

That's why money is allowed to live its own life in the dark.
It becomes a shadow we drag along without knowing it.

In this chapter, we'll learn to look at ourselves honestly—without shame, without hurry.

Because maybe it's not about what you can afford. Maybe it's about what you dare to take responsibility for—with gentleness.

When Money Becomes an Extension of Emotion. When We Pay to Avoid Feeling.

We say we "just needed something."
That it was on sale.
That it was a small thing.

But sometimes we don't buy the thing—we buy the feeling.
We buy comfort, validation, control, pause.

Gabor Maté has pointed out how addiction is often a strategy to regulate pain rather than a pursuit of pleasure.

Small financial behaviors can resemble addictive patterns—when they become automatic responses to discomfort. That doesn't make them wrong. But it makes them important to notice.

Maria and the Small Purchases That Spoke Louder

Maria had her finances in order. Paid on time. Had an overview.
And yet, there was rarely money left over.

She started writing down her daily purchases:
A coffee, a croissant, a hand cream, a flower, a new notebook.
Each with a small justification. A little comfort.

When she saw the list, it struck her:
'This isn't a strategy—it's emotional self-care disguised as spending.'

She had used money as language. A language for things she wasn't otherwise saying:
"I need care. I want to be felt."

Jonas and the Purchase That Was Never Unboxed

Jonas rarely bought anything—but when he did, it could be expensive.
One day, he walked into a store and bought a smartwatch.
Not because he needed it.
But because he felt overlooked.

His idea had been dismissed at work. A colleague got the credit.
And Jonas smiled and said nothing.

So he went and bought the watch.
But when he got home, he didn't open it.
It sat in the box for weeks.
As proof—not of wealth, but of pain.

When Money Hides What We Don't Have Words For

Maria and Jonas' examples aren't extreme.
They're everyday.
And that's exactly why they matter.

Because money can become a kind of emotional shortcut:

- We act before we feel.
- We avoid before we understand.

Daniel Kahneman described two thinking systems:
A fast, impulsive, emotionally driven one—and a slower, reflective one.
When we spend without thinking, it's often the fast system reacting.
Not because we're weak—but because we're overwhelmed.

The Shadow of Money—When We No Longer Want to Know

We hide. Delay. Leave the letters unopened.
For many, financial avoidance isn't laziness—it's shame.
Shame about not having control.
Shame about feeling incompetent.
Shame about not living up to one's own ideals.

And shame has a particular power:
It isolates us.
It makes us hide.
It makes action harder—even when we know what to do.

You could call it corruption with ourselves—when we break inner agreements silently. Agreements like:
'I won't spend more on that this month.'
'I'll check my account every Monday.'
'I'll pack lunch from now on.'

We make small internal contracts.
But we break them. Quietly.

And the worst part isn't the broken promise itself. It's that we lose connection with ourselves. That's how it is with all kinds of misuse—even the small ones.

We start thinking:

"It doesn't matter. I just can't get it together." And then self-respect slowly begins to erode.

Taking Yourself Seriously—Without Perfection

Taking yourself seriously doesn't mean always keeping your promises.

It means being willing to pause when you don't.

To look at it with curiosity—not blame.

We must ask ourselves:

- What happened?
- What need got in the way?
- What do I want to be more honest about with myself?

When we dare to look honestly—not harshly, but kindly—something else grows: *Self-respect.*

When Money Ends Up in the Basement

Here's a different image for the same issue—money that disappears into the dark.

It might be expenses we don't fully understand. Ones that creep in during the evening when we're tired, or on weekends when loneliness hits. Money that was supposed to bring value but didn't. Money that seems to serve another force. And maybe it does.

To understand this side of our spending, we must first admit that strong emotions are at play. Often around longing and wounds. Often about things we've tried to forget.

The psychoanalyst **Sigmund Freud** was the first to describe the *unconscious.* His image was that the mind is like a house. On the ground floor lives the *conscious self.* From here, we act, plan, shop, manage a budget—or try to.

But upstairs, on the first floor, lives the *superego*. The inner judge. The voice that says, "You can't do that," "That's irresponsible," or "You should have better control."

It's not always a pleasant voice. It was shaped by our upbringing, society's norms, and our own expectations. And it may be right. But it can also be harsh.

So what happens when we—as children, teens, or adults—feel something that doesn't fit into the superego's system?

We often try to get rid of it. We push it away. Down. Down into the basement.

There, in the house's dark lower level, lives *the unconscious*. The basement where we hide parts of ourselves we can't bear to see. The urge to spend impulsively. The dream of luxury after growing up with scarcity. The desire to reward ourselves—even if we "don't deserve it."

Everything we don't know how to handle—it ends up in the basement.

But what we push away lives on. It bangs on the pipes. It whispers from the corners. It guides the hand that clicks "buy now," even though we said we'd save. It's the hidden voice behind certain financial decisions—the ones we can't explain afterward.

So how do we approach it?

Not with scolding. Not with a new Excel template.

But with gentleness.

Steps Toward a More Honest and Conscious Finances:

Acknowledge That the Basement Exists

That you've hidden something doesn't mean you're wrong. It means you tried to survive. Our subconscious habits often began as defenses—not mistakes. They were created when something was too hard to carry. When you look at your money habits with kindness, something new can begin.

Listen to the Bangs in the Pipes

What happens right before you swipe your card? What mood are you in? What are you longing for? It takes practice to catch it. But sometimes a purchase masks sadness, boredom, or the need for comfort. If you can catch that moment, you can start to act differently—with awareness instead of automaticity.

Visit the Basement—in Daylight

Imagine going down there with a friendly flashlight. Not to clean it all at once, but to look around. What's hiding there? What parts of yourself have you packed away? What would happen if you brought one of them up and dusted it off?

Maybe you'll discover that what you thought was a weakness was actually a longing. A part of you that still needs something. And maybe you can find new ways to care for that part—without letting it control your bank card.

Exercise: My Financial Shadow Side

A quiet conversation with what you usually avoid.

- What do I avoid looking at in my finances?
- Note it without judgment—a bill, an account, a habit.
- What feels hard about looking at it?
- Shame? Exhaustion? Fear? Uncertainty?
- What does it say about me—and is it true?
- What story is stuck in this area?
- What would gentle honesty look like today?
- A small step, a sentence: "I choose to..."

You're not alone!

All people have blind spots.

But not everyone dares to look.

You are now.

And that in itself is a movement toward something more important than money:

Trust. Integrity. And a life with more awareness.

Chapter 6

FEELING RICH, REGARDLESS OF INCOME

On mental wealth, financial self-understanding, and the value of the invisible

Brick-Rich — Emotionally Poor

She lived in a townhouse with a private garden and low expenses. Great location. No debt. Everything many people dream of.

Still, she often stood in the supermarket with a knot in her stomach.

She put items back on the shelf, shaking her head. Not because she didn't have the money—but because it felt like she didn't.

'I know I own the house.
But it doesn't feel like my money.
It doesn't help me when I'm at the checkout.
That's where I feel poor.'
The statement lingered.
Because what does it really mean to be rich?

And what does it take to feel that way?

When Money Becomes Psychology — Not Accounting

Most of us think wealth is about numbers: salary, assets, retirement savings.

But reality is often more psychological than financial.

You can earn a lot and feel pressured.

You can earn little and feel free.

And you can—like the woman with the townhouse—own a lot and still feel deprived.

This chapter explores that paradox:

That financial security is rarely created by your bank statement alone—but by how you understand yourself in relation to money.

We ask questions like:

Why do some people feel financially secure—and others don't—on the same income?

Why do we forget to include our values in the equation?

And how do we recreate a financial narrative based on freedom, possibility, and respect—instead of control and shame?

Half Full or Half Empty?

Imagine two people with exactly the same financial situation. Same salary. Same fixed expenses. Same savings.

One feels stressed. The other feels privileged.

The difference rarely lies in the numbers. It lies in the perspective.

It's about comparisons, expectations—and the story we tell about ourselves.

'I should have more.'

'I'm actually doing fine.'

The difference doesn't begin in the bank. It begins in the mind.

Maria and the Two Equations

For months, Maria had felt financially pressured.

She had started a new job with a slightly higher salary, but the money disappeared quickly.

Everything felt overwhelming.

One day, she sat down and made two simple lists:

List 1: What I Can't Afford

- New clothes
- A trip south
- Dining out
- Home exercise equipment

List 2: What I've Paid For and Still Have

- Rent paid
- Healthy food
- Dental bill
- Child's extracurricular activities
- Savings of $50

When she looked at them, something started to shift.

'I may not have a surplus—but I have my foundation.'

It didn't change her numbers. But it changed the way she lived with them.

When Psychology Drives Finances

Two fields help us understand this phenomenon:
Positive psychology and behavioral economics.

Positive Psychology — Discovering Your Own Possibilities
There are many reasons to engage with money.

But one of the most beautiful is this:
Money can actually improve your quality of life.

This is where positive psychology comes in.

While classical psychology often focuses on flaws, wounds, and deficiencies, positive psychology turns its gaze to what works. It asks:

— What helps people thrive?
— What creates a sense of meaning and agency?
— How do we build on what we already have?

It's not about repressing problems or blindly 'thinking positive.'
Rather, it's about *discovering* and *activating* your resources.
And that applies especially to your relationship with money.

We all know the feeling of financial powerlessness. That something isn't enough. That something is missing. That we're not in control—and maybe never will be.

But positive psychology reminds us that our focus shapes our experience.
If we only see lack, we'll end up living in an internal reality of scarcity.
If instead we direct our attention to what we have—and what we can do—our feelings and behaviors change.

That's why a central principle is:

When we see our own resources at play, our sense of satisfaction grows—and so does our courage and motivation.

That doesn't mean we should ignore financial challenges.
But we can begin asking in a different way:

Instead of: *"What am I missing?"*
We can ask: *"What do I have that I can act from?"*

Positive psychology emphasizes what's called strength-based development. That means building change around the resources you already possess—rather than trying to fix flaws.

For example:
If you have a good eye for detail, that can be a strength in your financial planning.
If you're easily delighted by small things, it can reduce the need for large spending.
If you're empathetic, you can use it to foster constructive financial conversations in your family.

In practice, it means we don't have to wait until everything is perfect to make a change.
We can begin where we are—and discover that we already have something in our hands.

Research in positive psychology shows that well-being isn't just about external circumstances, but about our experience of meaning, mastery, and connection.
Those three elements also appear when we look at financial behavior:

Meaning: When we experience that our money is being used in alignment with our values, our satisfaction increases. (See the chapter on dreams and guiding stars).

Mastery: When we feel capable of managing our finances—even in small ways—our sense of self grows. (See the chapter on financial honesty and habits).

Connection: When we speak openly with others about money and feel understood and accepted, both the relationship and trust are strengthened. (See the chapter on love and money).

If you want to change your finances, it's helpful to ask:
What am I already good at?
What gives me energy?
When do I feel competent—including financially?
What has previously brought me joy without costing much?

By using these resources as a starting point, you can create small changes that feel meaningful and realistic—not as punishment, but as care.

When you shift your focus from lack to possibility, you change your emotional state—and thus your financial behavior.

You become more patient with yourself.

You become better at setting goals you actually want to pursue. And you may discover that financial growth isn't just about discipline—but also about hope.

Behavioral Economics — When We Don't Do What We 'Should'

For many years, economic theories were based on an idealized image of humans as rational and calculating. A person who chooses the most advantageous option when all possibilities are presented. This person has a name: *Homo economicus.*

The problem is—this person doesn't exist in reality.

Because we are not calculators. We are feeling, remembering, and longing beings. And our financial behavior reflects that. That's why behavioral economics emerged as a field to understand how people *actually* behave—not just how they *should* behave.

Behavioral economics blends psychology and economics and asks:

What makes us buy, save, give, or avoid?

What happens when emotions, habits, and social comparisons come into play?

Let's take a closer look at some of the most influential concepts:

Reference Point — (Daniel Kahneman & Amos Tversky, 1979)

We don't evaluate things in absolute numbers. We judge them relative to something else.

This is called a *reference point*—and it's often invisible.

If you're used to earning $6.000 and are offered a job paying $5.500, it will feel like a loss—even though it's objectively a good salary. On the other hand, going from $4.000 to $4.500 can feel like a win—even though the final amount is lower.

We are constantly comparing. With the past. With others. With our own expectations. And those comparisons shape our financial emotions far more than the numbers themselves.

Loss Hurts Twice as Much — (Loss Aversion — Kahneman & Tversky, 1979)

One of the most well-documented findings in behavioral economics is that *loss hurts more than gain feels good.*

Specifically: The pain of losing $50 is about twice as intense as the joy of winning $50.

This means we often avoid risks—not because we don't want to win, but because we're afraid to lose.

We say no to opportunities out of fear of losing something we already have.

This mechanism helps explain why we cling to bad habits—and why financial change can feel frightening, even when we rationally know it's the best thing for us.

Mental Accounting — (Richard Thaler, 1985)

Imagine you lose a $100 bill on the street. You're annoyed—but maybe you move on.

Now imagine you've just bought movie tickets for $100, but then lose them on the way in. Would you buy new tickets?

Most people say no in the latter case—but yes in the first.

This shows, as we've seen in a previous chapter, that we divide money into mental 'boxes.'

One for food. One for fun. One for vacation. One for bills.

And we behave differently depending on which box we think the money comes from—even if the money is objectively the same.

We might spend on expensive shoes without blinking—but hesitate at the grocery store when butter has gone up by half a dollar.

It's not logic. It's psychology.

A Mirror More Than a Chart

Behavioral economics reminds us that financial behavior isn't just about math—it's about people.

About fear and hope. About the past and comparisons. About impressions and patterns we don't always see clearly.

And perhaps the most important thing is this:

When we understand how we're influenced—we can begin to act a bit more freely.

We can reevaluate our habits, recognize the invisible boxes, and maybe choose a bit more consciously the next time we reach for our debit card.

What Does It Mean for You?

→ You can feel poor in the middle of abundance—if your reference point is your neighbor's standard.

→ You can experience loss, even when you've chosen something you believe in.

→ You can feel rich if you notice how much of your life is already working.

So the question isn't just: *'How much do I have?'*

But rather: *'How do I understand what I have?'*

And that's where the ability to feel rich—regardless of income—begins.

It's Not Just What You Have—But What You Can Do

The Indian economist and Nobel laureate **Amartya Sen** has greatly influenced the way we understand economics from a human perspective. He proposed a radically different approach to wealth and opportunity—not by focusing on the size of one's income, but on what one's resources enable:

"What matters is not what you have. What matters is what you can do with what you have."

In economic discussions, we often talk about resources, income, and property. It's assumed that if two people have the same amount of money, they also have the same opportunities. But that's not necessarily true, says Sen.

Imagine two people with the same monthly income. One is healthy, has access to public transport, and lives in a safe neighborhood. The other lives with an invisible disability, in an isolated village without access to healthcare, and spends half of their money on medicine. On paper, they have the same means—but in practice, their opportunities are very different.

That's why Sen suggests that instead of looking only at money and resources, we look at what he calls *capabilities*. It's about what a person can actually do and be with the resources available.

A financial situation isn't just a set of numbers. It's a framework for living. And freedom isn't just the absence of external constraints—it's the presence of real opportunities to live a life one has reason to value.

Applied to personal finance:
It means we shouldn't just ask: 'How much do I have?'
But instead: 'What do my finances allow me to do—in my life, with my circumstances?'
Do my finances give me peace of mind? Do they give me flexibility? Do they give me access to community, health, growth?

And even more importantly:
Am I using my money in ways that expand my possibilities—or limit them?

When we view finances through Sen's lens, it becomes clear that money itself is not freedom.

But it can be a tool for freedom—if we dare to ask ourselves what we truly want to use it for.

Maria and Her Sentence

Maria had a sentence she would say half-jokingly:

"I've never been good with money."

It seemed harmless.

But as she began to reflect on it, she realized it had shaped her finances for years.

She had:

- Avoided investing: 'That's just not me.'
- Skipped salary negotiations: 'I don't want to seem greedy.'
- Downplayed her savings: 'It's just luck.'

It wasn't her financial reality holding her back.

It was her self-narrative.

Jonas and the Feeling of Being 'the Responsible One'

Jonas had a grip on the numbers. But he never felt at ease.

His identity was tightly tied to the role of the stable one—the one who carried it all.

So when something went wrong—an unexpected bill, a broken car—it didn't just feel inconvenient. It felt like a failure.

He carried a story where financial pressure meant personal failure.

Even when it was life's randomness that struck.

Rewrite Your Story

Our story is shaped by upbringing, environment, experiences—and above all, by how we interpret them.

We can't change the first elements. What's done is done. But because our interpretation plays the decisive role, it's possible to rewrite the story.

With gentleness and curiosity—you can create a different version, one that actually aligns better with your real life.

It's not about *sugarcoating* the past. It's *identity in motion.*

The Dream of Financial Independence

We usually talk about money as something we need to buy things. But one of the most valued things money can offer is *freedom*.

Freedom to do all sorts of things, to *say no*, to *say yes*, to *control your time*, and to *be independent.*

The dream of becoming financially independent occupies many people. Myself included.

For a while, I watched a lot of YouTube videos about writing and publishing books. At first glance, they focused on technical topics. But most of them reflected a deeper dream—to earn enough money to create a life free from time and place.

From self-publishing, the focus shifted to all kinds of passive income, webshops, affiliate marketing, etc.

Suddenly, I found myself caught up in the wave—or dream—of *financial independence.*

And it took me a long time to recognize the paradox:

"I was already financially independent, but didn't feel it."

Every month, my pension is deposited into my account. We've settled in Argentina, a country with low living costs. We have no debt and no major fixed expenses. I already have the freedom those videos offered countless ways to achieve.

"And yet I sat there dreaming along—as if something was still missing."

It was paradoxical and thought-provoking. Why?

"I think I was still measuring my worth by whether I could earn money.

Not because I needed to—but because I had learned to understand myself through my productivity, which in turn was measured in money."

When Freedom Becomes Invisible

It's a classic pattern:

We work hard to achieve financial independence—but once we get there, we don't know how freedom feels.

Because we've learned to measure ourselves by:

- Activity
- Efficiency
- Economic output

In my case, I had to look at my freedom and rediscover its value.

What Is Freedom to You?

For some, freedom is the ability to travel.

For others, it's the ability to stay home.

Some want flexibility.

Others long for peace.

But regardless of the form, it requires one thing: 'That you dare to feel it.'

Freedom isn't just having the choice—it's daring to use it.

Your Money or Your Life

In the book '*Your Money or Your Life,*' **Vicki Robin** poses a central question:

"Is it worth spending one hour of your life energy on this particular thing?"

Her point is that money itself is not the goal—quality of life is the goal.

She helps us articulate the kind of freedom that's truly valuable. What do you want to use your time, your energy, your days for?

Because freedom isn't just being free from work. It's knowing what you want to put in its place.

It can be surprising and disappointing when freedom feels empty—especially if you've fought for it all your life.

Suddenly you're there—with the opportunity to do whatever you want—and you think: 'Now what?'

It's not a sign of failure.

But all transitions take time. And that sense of emptiness may simply mean that your inner identity is still catching up to your outer reality.

Maybe you, like me, have already achieved a high degree of freedom—you just need to recognize it, remember it, or dare to feel it.

Exercise — Your Mental Wealth Ledger

This exercise isn't about your retirement savings.

It's about what you own—and what has value—that may never have made it into your calculations.

Take your time. Grab a notebook. Or simply read and let your thoughts wander.

1. What do you physically own that gives you safety or freedom?
Do you have a place to live?
Do you own something that's yours? (car, home, tools, equipment...)
Do you have access to nature, space, peace?
Do you own items that can be used for something important or fun?

2. What skills and resources do you have access to?
Are you good with your hands?
Can you create, teach, repair, write, care, understand?
What life experiences do you have that others could learn from?

3. What in your network and daily life gives you financial security—without you thinking about it?
Do you have people who would help you in a crisis?
Do you have a partner, children, parents, neighbors who create a sense of support?
Do you have systems (public or private) that work in the background?

4. What choices have you made that show what you prioritize—also financially?
Have you changed jobs, homes, or lifestyle to gain more freedom?
Have you chosen not to spend money on things you don't believe in?
Have you created a life that reflects your values more than your status?

5. What might a new financial self-description sound like?
Write a short text—3—4 sentences—beginning with:
"I own more than I usually see, because..."
"My life is richer than it looks in numbers, because..."
"I choose to see my finances as an expression of..."

This exercise is not a replacement for budgets and realism.

But it's a counterbalance to the inner voice that only counts money—and never feels what makes it valuable.

Chapter Summary

We've met both Maria and Jonas in their different experiences with money—and we've seen how their feelings didn't necessarily match the numbers.

That's exactly what this chapter wanted to show:

That our mental wealth ledger is often far more crucial to our quality of life than our financial statement.

We can feel poor in the midst of wealth—if we forget to count the invisible. Property, relationships, time, and freedom are real resources, even if they don't appear in our daily awareness.

Our financial self-narrative governs more than we think.

Thankfully, it can be changed—with new words, new insights, and new values.

The mental wealth ledger exercise became a concrete way
to make hidden wealth visible—and thus active in our lives.

Chapter 7

FINANCES AS A LIFE DECISION

Do your finances support your values?

A Small Pause in the Narrative

There's something in the air. Not dramatic. Not a grand turning point with fanfare. More like the silence that follows a long conversation—where the words begin to settle, and something else, perhaps deeper, is allowed to take over.

That's where we are now. After chapters on shame and self-deception, judges and budgets, hidden resources and mental poverty—we've slowly moved toward a different realization: that finances isn't just about numbers, but about narratives. Not just about understanding what we have—but who we are.

Until now, we've looked at money from the inside. We've felt how money stirs emotions, how the past sneaks into our choices, and how freedom isn't just something you get—but something you have to learn to receive.

But now it's time to rise from the couch. Shake off our shoulders. Look ahead. Time to ask the question that's really been lying beneath the surface all along:

What do I want to use my life—and my money—for?

Not as a quick reflex, but as a real guiding star. A question that might not get a clear answer—but that can still begin to shape direction. Because finances isn't just something to understand. It's also something to shape.

From Survival to Life Choice

Most of us learn early that money is about getting by. Paying the bills, avoiding trouble, being responsible. And that's important. But at some point—often in adulthood—another question arises:

If I'm not just here to survive—what am I really living for?

This is when finances begins to change character. It shifts from a battleground to a map. No longer just a question of how much you have, but of which direction you want to go.

A job can give you money—but also take your time.

A loan can open doors—but also tie you down.

A purchase can bring joy—but maybe also cost you freedom.

So what matters most?

This is where finances becomes a life language. A language where every dollar—and every choice—says something about who you are and what you prioritize. A language that can speak honestly or confusedly. Consciously or on autopilot.

In this chapter, we begin to view finances as an *active choice*, a *life story*. Not because we have control over everything—but because we have influence over what we want to stand for.

Maybe it's no longer about making the money stretch.

Maybe now it's about *making life stretch—and letting the money follow.*

Financial Integrity — Living by What You Believe In

We rarely hear the word integrity used with finances. Maybe because it sounds too solemn. Something for saints or philosophers. But in reality, financial integrity is a deeply human concept.

It's not about being perfect.

It's about asking yourself:

Am I living—including financially—in alignment with my values?

For some, that's about sustainability. For others, freedom. For some, it's the ability to give back. And for many, a mix—without having put precise words to it.

This is where financial integrity can function as a compass. Not a rulebook, but a *guiding star*:

What matters to me—and can I see that reflected in how I use my money?

Vicki Robin, author of *Your Money or Your Life*, suggests we ask whether our money serves our life.

Morgan Housel, in 'The Psychology of Money,' reminds us that most financial decisions are really about hope, fear, and identity.

So in this chapter, we don't ask:

How do you make it all add up?

But rather:

What kind of life are you trying to build—and how can your money help support that?

It doesn't require you to change jobs, open a new account, or overhaul your life. But it does require an eye for what you already believe in—and the courage to stand by it.

Jonas and Maria — Two Paths, Same Question

Jonas wakes up early these days. Not because he has anything urgent to do, but because his thoughts start spinning before the light hits the wall. Recently, he was offered a new job. More pay, more responsibility, more speed—and less space. On paper, a win.

But something feels off. Not fear, but a kind of inner noise. A restlessness that doesn't go away, even when he tries to convince himself it's "the right thing."

He writes in his notebook:

"If money weren't the problem—would I take the job?"

He doesn't know. But he knows the question isn't just about finances. It's about how he wants to live his life.

Maria, somewhere else in the city, gets a message from Sille, an old friend she hasn't seen in years. Sille lives in a commune outside town and invites Maria to visit. Maria hesitates, but says yes.

The next day, she's in a kitchen filled with the smell of homemade bread and the sound of shouting children in the background. Everything is used, uneven, and imperfect—and yet something about it feels good. A rhythm. A warmth. The finances isn't the center. It's there, but not in charge.

On the train ride home, Maria thinks:

"Maybe I've been striving for something I never actually chose myself."

Jonas and Maria don't know each other. But their questions are starting to resemble one another's. They both sense that financial decisions aren't just about money—but about identity, direction, and self-respect.

And maybe this is where something new begins:

That they—each in their own way—start to discover what they truly long for.

And What About You, Reader? You've come this far. (Well done!)

You've read about Jonas's doubts, Maria's discoveries, shadows and cracks. Maybe something resonated. A feeling. A choice. A longing.

Maybe you thought: "That could be me."

Maybe a thought arose that you haven't quite been able to shake.

But now it's not just about them. You are, in fact, the main character. So let me ask you some of the questions Jonas and Maria have started pondering:

What financial choices have you made that were really life choices?

Have you said yes to something you didn't believe in—because of financial pressure?

Or said no to something important—because it seemed unrealistic or "unreasonable" financially?

What dreams have you packed away because you couldn't see how they'd pay off?

And what investments—in yourself, your values, your freedom—have you perhaps not even noticed yet?

Asking yourself these questions doesn't mean you've done something wrong.

It means you're starting to see clearly.

That you're lifting your finances out of everyday automation—and beginning to listen to what they can also reveal about you.

We don't always have the freedom to choose freely.

But we almost always have the right to ask the question:

"How do I want to use my money—if it's also meant to tell a story about the life I wish to live?"

This isn't the end. It's the beginning of a new way of asking.

Not just: *"Can I afford this?"*

But also: *"Is this worth living for?"*

When the Mind Plays Tricks on Your Finances

We often believe we make financial decisions rationally. But as Daniel Kahneman and other behavioral economists have shown, the reality is more complex.

We don't just think with our heads.

We think with habits, hopes, fears, and old experiences.

And that means many financial choices are shaped by unconscious patterns—even when we believe we're being rational.

Four Common Psychological Biases

Status Quo Bias — We Stay Where We Are, Even If We're Unhappy

Status quo bias refers to our tendency to stick with the familiar—even when it's no longer serving us well. We often choose the safe, the known, the existing—simply because it feels less risky than change.

It's not necessarily the best choice. But it feels safe. It requires less energy or courage. Because what if the new thing turns out worse?

Example:

Jonas is considering quitting a job he doesn't enjoy. He can afford a break and dreams of doing something else. But the idea of stepping into the unknown makes him nervous. So he stays—even though every Monday he wakes up with a knot in his stomach.

Status quo bias makes us overestimate the value of what we already have—and underestimate the possibilities in what we haven't yet tried. It can hold us back from taking steps that might bring us closer to the life we truly want.

The known feels safer than the unknown. Even when the known no longer works.

Loss Aversion — We Hate Losing More Than We Love Winning

Loss aversion describes the psychological phenomenon that we react more strongly to losses than to gains. Research shows we typically experience a loss as twice as painful as a corresponding gain is joyful.

This means we often make decisions based on avoiding loss—even if it stands in the way of something we long for.

Example:

Maria has saved $10.000. She could use some of it to take a course she's long dreamed of—one that might open new doors. But she can't bring herself to do it. Just the thought of the balance shrinking feels like a loss. So she holds back—and feels disappointed afterward.

Loss aversion can make us cling to what feels safe, even when something else might be more valuable in the long run. It can hold us back—without us realizing it.

Confirmation Bias — We Look for Proof of What We Already Believe

If we've learned that financial responsibility means a full-time job and a pension, we'll struggle to see the value in anything that doesn't fit that image.

Some people reject flexible working lives—not because they're bad, but because they clash with their core narrative.

Future Blindness — We Assume We'll Stay the Same

We often plan as if we'll never change. But we do. Our values, dreams, and needs evolve over time.

A long-term savings plan might eventually lead to something we no longer want—simply because we didn't adjust our course along the way.

These psychological patterns aren't flaws in us.

They're natural—but they require awareness. Only when we notice them can we begin to choose differently—not necessarily smarter, but more honestly.

From Automatic Choices to Conscious Decisions

Jonas had never asked himself why he always said yes to the safe option.

Maria had never considered why her budgets were so detailed they resembled control sheets.

They did what they thought was right.

Because it's what they'd learned.

Because it seemed responsible.

But beneath it all were automatic patterns. And that's not abnormal—it's human.

Most financial decisions are made on autopilot. We follow habits, impulses, the culture around us—or our own old beliefs.

We say yes because we're used to it. Or no because we're afraid.

But what happens when we pause and ask:

'Why am I actually doing it this way?'

It doesn't require becoming a financial expert. But it does require awareness. And the courage to explore when we're acting from habit—and when we're acting from conscious choice.

Questions That Open the Door to More Conscious Decisions

1. When did I say yes but mean no?

— A job, a gift, an investment, a commitment?

— What did I agree to out of guilt, habit, or expectation—not conviction?

2. What would I choose if I weren't afraid?

— If the fear of loss, disappointment, or judgment didn't control the decision—what would I choose?

3. How would I use my money if no one judged me?

— Would I spend it differently?

— Would I allow myself more play, more rest, more quirkiness?

Conscious choices aren't necessarily the most 'right' in the traditional sense. They're not always the most profitable or efficient. But they align better with the life you want to live.

Shift in Perspective — Finances as Character Development

Imagine your financial life isn't just a spreadsheet—but a script.

Every time you spend money, you write a small scene.

When you save, you're editing the next act.

When you change a spending habit, you revise your role.

And when you say no to something, you're also saying yes to something else—often something invisible, but meaningful.

It requires a shift in perspective.

Not from irresponsibility to responsibility.

But from function to narrative.

A New Look at Saving

Maria experienced this shift one day when she looked at her savings and asked:

"What do these funds really represent for me?"

Previously, the answer had been: security.

But now she saw something else: trust.

Trust that her future is worth investing in. That she would give herself something later—even though she didn't yet know what it was.

The savings weren't just an amount, but a sign that she believes in her own life.

A New Look at Saying No

Jonas felt the same shift when he turned down the new job. At first, he saw it as a loss—something he had to give up. But instead, it felt like protection of something vulnerable and important within himself.

Something he wanted to take care of.

He realized that financial choices are also character choices.

Saying no can be an act of courage—not fear.

Saving money can be a sign of freedom—not stinginess.

Spending money on something impractical can be a tribute to beauty, play, or hope.

Conclusion — Your Finances as Life Story

You've now followed Jonas and Maria through a series of choices, doubts, and emerging insights. Maybe you've recognized something in them.

This chapter has shown us three layers of financial decisions:

- Structural choices: What kind of life do I want to build, and how does the finances fit in?
- Relational choices: How does money affect my close relationships?
- Existential choices: What do my financial choices say about who I am—and who I want to be?

The most important point is that *conscious choices are possible.*

First comes awareness—of conscious and unconscious patterns, to understand why we do what we do.

Then come the questions about our practice. Do our habits align with our identity—does our finances support the life we want to live?

Finally, we become capable of making new and more conscious choices.

Chapter 8

ON TRUE AND FALSE SECURITY

Do you have the courage to trust yourself?

Everything Was in Place — Except the Peace

He sat at the dining table in the house he had lived in for the past 37 years.

A cup of coffee sat untouched beside him, and in front of him lay the letter from the pension fund.

There was nothing surprising about it—he had run the numbers himself long ago. He could retire now. He should.

And yet… he wasn't sure.

He had done everything right.

Saved. Invested cautiously. Bought stocks at the right time and kept them until they showed a profit. Paid off the house early. Stayed out of consumer debt. Never lived beyond his means.

He had always had one goal: *to secure himself.* To have the power to choose. To stand free when the time came.

And now he sat here.

And felt... *uneasy*.

He tried to think rationally. The bank statement told one story: *security*.

But his body told another. His chest was tight, as if something were about to happen. But nothing happened. Just silence. Just time, passing.

He thought back on all the years he had spoken of everything he would do.

'Someday,' he had said. 'When I'm free.' But now freedom wasn't a door opening. It was an abyss. An unfamiliar emptiness.

Maybe he had always used his money and his plans as a shield. A protection against what he didn't have words for—uncertainty, freedom, the openness of life. He realized that *security* had been his lifeboat.

But now that he could go ashore, it was the very ground beneath him he no longer trusted.

He had nothing left to fight for. And maybe that was the scariest part of all.

Financial Security Is Not the Same as Inner Safety

The story of the man at the table is far from unusual. On the contrary. It points to one of the great paradoxes in modern economic thinking:

'That financial security does not necessarily create inner safety.'

We've been taught that saving, investing, and securing the future is the path to freedom. But for many—especially when the goal is finally reached—a strange emptiness arises. A sense that something is missing. Not in the account, but in the body.

Security turns out to be more than a number. More than bricks and savings. Security is a feeling. An experience. A trust—that cannot be bought.

So what is it we're really seeking when we say we want financial security? And why can it feel so unsafe to receive what we've longed for?

This chapter is not about canceling your pension savings or living without a safety net. It's about examining what security actually consists of—and how we relate to it.

This aspect deserves an entire chapter—and a long one at that. Because it plays a significant role for many of us.

We'll take a closer look at how psychological mechanisms like 'fear of loss,' 'status quo bias,' and 'illusion of control' can lead us to cling to external safety—without experiencing inner peace.

We'll meet people who have 'enough,' but don't feel it. And we'll explore how we can attain inner calm—without deceiving ourselves.

The goal is not to abandon security, but to make it human. And to open a new door in our understanding:

That true security may not only be about money—but about the courage to trust ourselves.

When Everything Is in Place — And Nothing Feels Safe

When people talk about financial security, most think of something concrete: A stable job. A pension. A house that's paid off.

Money in the account to cover three months of expenses—or preferably six.

It's about being able to withstand unforeseen events. To be prepared. To stand firm in a storm. And that makes sense.

Financial security is not an illusion. It means being able to breathe a little easier, make decisions with more calm, and say yes or no to something without panicking.

But it's not the same as psychological safety.

Psychological safety is not about what we have—but how we *experience* what we have. It's about the inner state we carry with us:

Whether we dare believe that the world won't collapse if we loosen our grip a little.

Whether we believe we can handle it if something unexpected happens.

Whether we feel we're allowed to be here—even if we're not performing, saving, or 'doing the right thing.'

Psychological safety, in other words, isn't tied to our online bank account—but to our fundamental experience of ourselves in the world.

And here's the problem. Many try to achieve inner peace through financial safety. But it only works partially.

You can have a solid financial foundation—and still feel uneasy.

You can have 'enough'—and still think: 'It's not certain.'

The relationship between financial and psychological safety is therefore *asymmetrical*:

One can support the other—but they can't replace each other.

You can't calculate your way to inner peace. And you can't save your way out of existential uncertainty.

Inner Filters and Perceptions

Our experience of security passes through a filter. Not an objective filter—but a personal, emotional, and historically shaped layer of experiences, beliefs, culture, and upbringing.

It's this filter that determines whether '$15.000 in the bank' feels like freedom—or like the beginning of a catastrophe we haven't yet named.

For some people, the inner filter is colored by frugality and responsibility. They've learned that money should be saved—not spent.

Others carry an inner voice that says you must always be prepared for the worst. That life can change in an instant—and that peace is something you can only allow yourself when everything is secure. Which it rarely is.

We also form ideas about what 'enough' is. But that 'enough' keeps moving. As we approach it, it shifts a little farther away. We compare ourselves to others—their homes, pensions, choices—and feel our own situation is inadequate, even when it's objectively solid.

Some beliefs are nearly invisible:

'You mustn't be a burden to anyone.'

'You should manage on your own.'

'You must never be dependent on others.'

These beliefs rarely sit at the front of our minds—but they govern our decisions. They make us save more, delay pleasures, decline help—not because it's necessary, but because it feels right.

Or at least: safe.

And here we encounter one of the greatest paradoxes:

'The feeling of safety often doesn't come when we've secured ourselves.'

It only emerges when we begin to understand how we see ourselves—and why we believe we must be more prepared than everyone else.

In earlier chapters, we explored the classic psychological biases—our tendencies to overestimate losses, stick with the familiar, and repeat patterns without recognizing them.

But here we're getting closer to something else. Something deeper. Namely the question:

'*What is it in us that makes it hard to feel safe—even when everything is in place?*'

In the next section, we'll look at some of the existential and emotional mechanisms that hold us back:

Our relationship with control—and the fear of losing it.

Our experiences with loss and trust—and how past betrayals color today's decisions.

Our self-image as responsible, worthy, financially mature adults—and how fragile that image really is.

We move from cognitive explanations to something more human and embodied. To the part of finances that's about identity, self-perception, and the feeling of belonging.

And precisely there—in the soft, imprecise, and personal—we might find a different kind of security.

One that can't be measured—but can be felt.

When Safety Was Never Learned

He couldn't say exactly why, but he had always had a hard time relaxing.

Even as an adult with a steady job, a solid financial footing, a house of his own, and bills paid on time—something never quite settled.

It was as if there was a small, watchful animal inside him that never slept. An instinct, a tension that whispered:

"You can't stop. Something might happen. It's all on you."

According to Hungarian-Canadian physician and author **Gabor Maté**, the situation above isn't abnormal—but *unresolved.*

He points out that many of us carry deep wounds from childhood—without necessarily labeling them trauma in the traditional sense.

It's not just about what happened—but about what was missing:

Presence. Care. Predictability. An adult's ability to say: "You are safe, and you're allowed to be as you are."

If you didn't learn safety as a child, you won't have access to it as an adult—not even if you have enough money.

Maté writes that we develop what he calls 'adaptive survival strategies'—patterns that helped us navigate unpredictable environments in childhood, but later in life become rigid, controlling, or self-suppressing.

An adult who has a grip on their finances but still feels discomfort spending money on themselves may not be stingy. They may simply never have learned to feel safe.

What we call control, responsibility, or self-discipline in adulthood may in fact be a thin layer of order laid over an old sense of helplessness.

If, as a child, you experienced that things could vanish from one day to the next—a fight, a parent who disappeared into silence or anger, a shaky household finances—you may have learned that safety is dangerous.

That you mustn't relax.

That you must be prepared.

That you must always be alert.

When Finances Becomes a Shield—or a Prison

And so our understanding of finances naturally becomes shaped—as a means of gaining control, a shield, and sometimes a prison.

Something we use to keep uncertainty at bay—and to make sure we never lose balance again.

Maté highlights that many people use performance, control, and self-denial as ways to avoid the pain they once felt.

But these strategies—even when they lead to financial success—come at a cost. They keep us trapped in an old worldview, where peace must be earned through effort, and self-care is something only allowed once everything else is in place.

Freedom—including financial freedom—requires something else:

That we dare to meet the unrest we carry and acknowledge that it stems from a place where we didn't get what we needed. And that we—now as adults—can begin to give ourselves what we never got then:

Calm. Compassion. Permission to simply exist.

Taking Up Space in Your Financial Life

Maria had avoided buying new clothes for years. She told herself it wasn't necessary. That it was more 'financially responsible' not to.

But one day, as she stood in the fitting room wearing a dress she really liked, she felt a strange unease. As if the mirror didn't just reflect the dress—but also an old inner voice saying:

'That's not you. You're not allowed to wear that.'

She ended up putting the dress back. Not because she lacked the money. But because something in her didn't have *permission.*

This is where **Amy Cuddy**'s concept of *embodied confidence* comes in—the idea that our sense of worth doesn't live only in our thoughts, but also in our bodies, our posture, and our way of inhabiting the world.

Cuddy distinguishes between *dominance* and *personal power.*

It's not about dominating others—but about being able to feel your own space, fill it, and be present within yourself.

Presence, she writes, 'is the state of being attuned to and able to comfortably express our true thoughts, feelings, values, and potential.'

When someone—like Maria—has learned throughout life that they must take up little space, not disturb, not cost anything, it becomes hard to allow themselves to spend money. Even if they have it.

Financial freedom becomes something you have—but don't dare to use.

Cuddy suggests that access to financial worthiness often starts in the body. Not with a big leap, but with small physical adjustments:

Standing up straighter. Speaking a bit more clearly. Taking up more room.

And from there—little by little—beginning to make choices that reflect that new bodily grounding.

Maria's story isn't unusual.

Many people—especially women—carry an inner conflict between financial capacity and the feeling of being worthy of using it.

They may have a good job, a savings account, a sensible spending pattern—and still feel that they 'shouldn't enjoy anything.'

But worthiness is not something others grant you. It's something you practice returning home to.

When we dare to take up space in our financial lives—with dignity and presence—safety begins to feel real. Not because everything is in order. But because we've finally landed in ourselves.

The Inner Straitjacket — Control as a Substitute for Trust

Some people create budgets down to the last decimal, update spreadsheets weekly, and know their pension rate better than their own pulse. It can look like sound financial responsibility—and maybe it is. But in some cases, it's something else. Something more intense. Something more desperate.

When control becomes a straitjacket meant to hold together a deeper anxiety, money takes on a new role. It's no longer just a practical tool—but a way to keep the world at a distance.

People who have experienced loss, unpredictability, or emotional absence in childhood often develop a strong need for control.

They've learned that it's not safe to trust someone will catch them. That help may not come.

That responsibility—always—ends with them.

So control becomes more than a habit—it becomes a life strategy. A shield. A system designed to reduce the risk of disappointment—and that also limits access to spontaneity, joy, and freedom.

This might sound like excessive psychologizing. But most people recognize the feeling: That it's easier to manage the budget than to feel uncertainty. That it's safer to stay in a secure but unsatisfying job than to take a chance and apply elsewhere. That it feels better to go without something than to risk being left with nothing.

It's as if the body says:

'Better a little and safe—than a lot and uncertain.'

But there's a cost.

When financial control becomes a substitute for trust, we risk losing touch with life's more vibrant and spontaneous rhythms.

We forget to ask:

"What do I actually want?"

We ignore the inner signals that speak of dreams, desire, longing, and need—and listen only to the voice that demands control.

This can lead to a life that looks sensible from the outside—but feels tight and rigid from within. A life where we do everything right—but rarely feel joy. Where we're constantly securing ourselves—but never feel secure.

I'm not suggesting we abandon structure—but that we dare ask ourselves an honest question:

"What exactly am I trying to protect?" And: "Are there other ways to create security—ways that don't bind me, but build me up?"

When Safety Begins from Within

When we begin to understand that financial security is shaped by our inner stories, our bodies, and our emotional inheritance, new possibilities emerge.

We can start to ask ourselves: *"How does safety feel in me?"*

And: *"What do I need to know, feel, and believe—in order to be able to receive it?"*

For many, the next step will be to notice and understand the patterns we carry. Because behind every pattern lies protection. Something we once needed. Something that may once have held us up—but now holds us back.

Here, the voices of Gabor Maté and Amy Cuddy are not solutions, but guiding lights. They bring clarity to what we're really reacting to when we think it's about money.

Maté helps us recognize internal tensions as lived experience. He reminds us that control often hides an old wound—and that healing begins when we meet it with kindness.

Cuddy shows us that even with a long history of self-limitation, we can begin to take up space again. That dignity and financial freedom don't require permission from others—but begin in the body, in the voice, in the way we move through a room.

When we dare to acknowledge where we come from—and begin to practice standing in who we are—security can become something other than the absence of danger. It can become an inner movement. A place of rest. A quiet nod to oneself that says:

"I'm here—and I'm allowed to be.

That's what the next section is about. How to begin—not with perfection, but with movement. With building a kind of security that not only protects—but makes space for life.

Maria and Jonas in the Field

We've met Maria and Jonas before—each with their own way of struggling with money. They've known anxiety, control, inner voices that either pressure or silence them.

But this time we don't meet them in conflict. We meet them in everyday life. In the small, almost invisible moments when something begins to shift. When old patterns don't disappear, but get disrupted. When a new sentence sneaks in and stays. Not as a revolution, but as a different way of being in oneself.

Maria hadn't actually planned to buy anything. She'd just stepped into the bookstore to wait for the bus because it was raining and she didn't want to stand outside. But there—on one of the front tables—lay a book she'd looked at several times before. One of those you don't need, but still long for.

She picked it up, turned it over, read the back cover again, even though she nearly knew it by heart. It was about something she couldn't quite explain—something about slowness, about coming home to yourself.

She looked at the price. $45. Not unreasonable. But not pocket change either. She felt the familiar sting. The inner voice that said:

"It's not necessary."

"You already have enough books."

"What if you need the money for something more important?"

She put the book back. Walked around a bit. Looked at pens, postcards, a calendar she didn't need. But her eyes kept returning to the book.

Something strange happened. Not a rebellion—not a big decision.

More like a gentle, inner sentence that appeared without drama:

"I'm allowed."

She didn't say it out loud. But she felt it. And she picked the book up again. This time not to consider—but to walk up to the counter.

Out in the rain, she carried it in a small paper bag. And it wasn't just a book she was holding—it was a practice in trust.

A reminder that security sometimes begins with giving yourself permission for something small.

It was really just a coincidence.

Jonas was tidying up his digital files one morning when he came across an old insurance policy he had almost forgotten. An extended accident policy he had taken out years ago—shortly after his mother passed away, when he had first truly felt how fragile life could be.

Back then, it had made sense. He had been alone, vulnerable, and wanted to ensure that if something happened, he wouldn't become a burden.

The policy had felt like an invisible hand on his back.

A reassurance: "You've planned ahead."

But now, as he reread the terms, he felt oddly detached from it all. His life looked different now. His finances were solid. His view of risk more realistic. And yet he had never canceled the policy. Maybe because it had become a symbol. A quiet promise to himself to be responsible.

He closed his eyes for a moment. Asked himself what he would do

if he trusted that he was okay. Not invincible. Not protected against everything. But simply… okay.

And with that thought, he opened the insurance company's website. Found the cancellation form. Entered his details.

Paused before clicking "send."

For a moment he thought: "Is this foolish? Irresponsible? Am I gambling with my future?"

But then another sentence came to him—almost an echo of what Maria had felt the day before: "Maybe it's also responsible to trust that I don't need all the extras."

He clicked "send."

It wasn't a revolution. He was still sitting in his living room, surrounded by coffee, paper piles, and midmorning light. But something had changed. He had let go. Not of safety—but of an old form of control. And it felt like a small victory. Not just for his finances—but for the way he lived in the world.

Exercise: My Personal Safety Ledger

Imagine creating not just a financial budget—but a safety ledger. An overview, not of your money, but of your sense of security.

What makes you feel calm?

What makes you tense up?

Where in your life do you feel covered—and where do you sense gaps?

This exercise is not about how much you have in your account or how well you've invested. It's about noticing what feels safe and what feels unsafe—regardless of what the numbers say.

The purpose of this exercise is to: Raise awareness of your inner sources of safety—both those you may overlook and those you may overvalue.

Challenge the idea that financial security is only about external guarantees.

Connect with what actually makes you stronger, calmer, and more free.

We'll explore five areas of your life where safety plays a role:

- Your finances
- Your relationships
- Your home and daily life
- Your inner psychological resilience
- Your dreams and sense of agency

Instructions:

Take your time. You don't need to complete everything at once. You can focus on one area at a time—and come back later. The most important thing is to answer honestly. Not based on how you should feel, but on how you actually feel.

Use a notebook, and write more than a word. Some answers require sentences—not numbers.

Reflection and Journaling Across Five Life Areas

1. Finances — What do I know, and what do I feel?

- What makes me feel financially calm—in concrete, practical terms?
- What makes me feel unsafe, even when I know I have things under control?
- Are there areas of my finances where I overreact—or avoid facing reality?
- What old beliefs are driving my financial behavior?

Reflection:

Where I feel strong:

→ …

Where I feel uneasy:

→ …

A new phrase I want to practice thinking:

→ …

2. Relationships — Who holds me?

- Who can I talk to when I feel unsafe?
- Do I tend to withdraw when I'm uncertain—or seek reassurance?
- Is there anyone I struggle to share financial concerns with—and why?

Reflection:

A secure relationship:

→ …

A missing connection or support:

→ …

Something I want to try reaching out about:

→ …

3. Home and Daily Life — What space holds my safety?

- Do I feel safe in my home? Does it feel like my place?
- Is there something in my daily life that brings stability—or something that disrupts it?
- Does my physical space give me calm—or drain my energy?

Reflection:

Where I feel at ease:

→ …

What creates inner restlessness in my environment:

→ …

A small change I want to try:

→ …

4. Inner Resilience — What do I carry within myself?

- What have I overcome that I often forget to recognize?
- What do I tell myself when things get hard—and would I say the same to a friend?
- Do I have moments in everyday life where I feel strong, worthy, or brave?

Reflection:

My strength is:

→ …

My inner straitjacket sounds like this:

→ …

A new way I want to speak to myself:

→ …

5. Dreams and Agency — What do I dare to believe in?

- What dreams have I pushed away using financial arguments?
- Do I dare imagine a life where I feel free—not just safe?
- What could be one small step toward something that feels more true?

Reflection:

A dream I've tucked away:

→ …

Something I want to take one step toward:

→ …

A "just for fun" choice that could create movement:

→ …

Closing Reflection: What surprised me?

Was there an answer that caught me off guard?

Were there areas where I feel stronger than I expected?

Was there something I want to take seriously in a new way?

Free notes:

→ …

Closing the Exercise: Your Safety Ledger Is in Motion

You've now reflected on five areas of your life where safety either shows up—or hides. Perhaps you've discovered patterns you hadn't noticed before. Maybe you've realized that safety isn't just about protecting yourself from the unpredictable—but about standing up for yourself and your needs.

Remember:

A safety ledger is not static. It's not a one-time task. It's something you can revisit, adjust, and revise—just like life changes. You're not behind because you feel insecure. You're already on your way—because you've started listening.

Safety as a Life Decision

Safety is not a guarantee. It's not a reward for doing everything right. It's a decision. A life choice. A mindset toward yourself and what you're living through. And like every decision, there will be moments when you forget. When you slip back into old patterns. When fear takes over again. When you think:

"Maybe it's too soon."
"Maybe I should have waited."
"Maybe it's not enough."

But that's precisely when the decision matters most. Not as something dramatic—but as a quiet inner sentence:

"I return."
"I choose it again."
"I won't wait to feel safe."

Because you've already started the journey. You've felt something shift inside you. Maybe just a glimpse—a new sentence, a small act, a book, a conversation, a decision you no longer fear.

And that's what makes it a life decision. Not that it's easy.
But that you've chosen to live with dignity—even in imperfection.

That you've chosen to build safety from the inside out— not just wait for it to come from the outside.

You'll forget it.
You'll remember it.
But you can always choose it again.
Safety you choose for yourself is something no one can take away.

Chapter Summary

This chapter has explored a paradox: That one can have financial security—and still feel unsafe. And the reverse: That even in uncertainty, one can begin to build inner peace.

We followed Jonas and Maria in their reflections, and we introduced theories from Gabor Maté and Amy Cuddy, which point to how inner safety is about connection, self-worth, and social grounding—not just external control.

We worked with a personal safety ledger that helps clarify where safety lives in your life—and where it may be missing.

And finally:
A life decision.

That safety isn't something to wait for. It's something to choose. Again and again. With dignity. With calm. With yourself by your side.

Chapter 9

MONEY AND PERSONALITY

Who are you in financial disguise?

Financial Personality Types — With a Wink

There are many ways to categorize people. But sometimes, a little self-irony and lightheartedness can help us see ourselves—and each other—more clearly.

Here are five informal but recognizable financial personality types. You might see yourself in one of them. Or two. Or all of them—depending on your mood. That's okay. It's not about fitting into a box. It's about discovering your own financial language.

1. The Planner

"I have a spreadsheet for everything. And a color-coded system to find it."

The Planner loves an overview. The budget isn't a burden—it's a friend. Everything has its place: accounts, cash, categories.

Planners feel calm knowing what's coming in and going out—preferably with projections. They feel secure when the future is mapped out. But they may struggle to let go and just do something spontaneous. Unpredictability doesn't feel like freedom—it feels like a threat.

2. The Bon Vivant

"You only live once—and today is a great excuse."

The Bon Vivant lives in the moment, and money is for creating experiences, joy, and ambiance. A nice meal, a spontaneous weekend trip, a new dress, a gift 'just because.'

Bon Vivants usually don't mind spending money—but they'd rather not spend much time talking about it. Just the thought of a budget feels overwhelming and kills the vibe.

They're not irresponsible—they're just more afraid of missing out on life than of losing **money.**

3. The Minimalist

"If I don't need it, I don't want to own it."

The Minimalist lives simply and thrives with few belongings, clear boundaries, and peace of mind. Rarely spends money—and when they do, it's deliberate.

It may seem austere, but to the Minimalist, it's not deprivation—it's freedom.

They know their needs and stick to them. But they may miss out on joy because they fear losing control or balance.

4. The Protector

"The most important thing is that everyone else is okay."

The Protector spends money on others before themselves. They buy gifts, treat people, and say 'I'll get this one.'

They feel responsible and find meaning in caring for others. But sometimes they go beyond their limits.

They forget themselves in the desire to create safety—and can become resentful if not met with gratitude. They need to realize that care also includes themselves.

5. The Freedom Lover

"As long as I'm not tied down—I'll be fine."

Freedom Lovers have a complicated relationship with money. They crave independence—and financial systems feel like traps.

Budgets, savings goals, retirement plans: all seem like threats to spontaneity.

They're often creative, resourceful, and good at finding solutions when money is tight. But they may also avoid financial responsibility—because it stirs up old feelings of control or helplessness.

No type is better than another

We all carry strengths and vulnerabilities—even in our financial lives. The most important thing isn't to become a new type. It's to understand your own patterns—and to recognize that they can be adjusted if they're standing in the way of the life you want to live.

When two financial languages meet

It's one thing to understand yourself. It's something entirely different to be confronted with someone who reacts completely differently to the exact same situation.

When that happens—in a romantic relationship, a friendship, or a family—money becomes more than just a practical necessity. (We'll return to that in a later chapter.)

Money becomes a language. And like all languages, there's a risk of misunderstanding if you don't know each other's dialects.

So let's return to Jonas and Maria—two people who both want to live meaningfully and responsibly, but who have very different financial temperaments.

Jonas and Maria — two financial temperaments living parallel lives

Jonas has always needed structure. Even as a boy, he created systems for his savings: a box with three compartments, small labels, and amounts written in ballpoint pen.

As an adult, he works methodically—in both his job and his finances. He keeps a budget, does monthly status updates, and knows exactly how much he has left over after all fixed expenses and savings goals are met.

To him, money means security—not just for today, but for the future. He feels calm when the numbers add up. Unexpected expenses make his shoulders tense—not because he's stingy, but because uncertainty feels threatening.

Money isn't just a tool—it's a form of anchoring.

Maria has a different rhythm. She's not irresponsible—on the contrary. But her approach to money is more intuitive. She creates life around her: happily buys a coffee, invites people to dinner, purchases something beautiful for the home—even if it wasn't on any list.

Systems feel restrictive to her—not because she doesn't understand them, but because they quickly start to feel like straightjackets. When she has surplus, she feels it in her body and acts on it. When finances are tight, she finds creative solutions. She's learned to navigate periods of irregular income, and her financial style is marked by adaptability and trust—even when the future is unclear.

Jonas and Maria live their lives in very different ways. They don't know each other. But if they did, they might be puzzled by each other's choices—or maybe intrigued.

Because behind the differences aren't conflicting values—but different ways of creating safety, freedom, and meaning in life.

When personality gets in the way—and how to loosen the knot

There's nothing wrong with being a planner. And nothing wrong with being spontaneous. But problems can arise when we don't understand the difference—or when we try to follow a financial method that doesn't suit who we really are.

Jonas feels unsafe when money changes hands quickly. He can get so focused on preparing that he forgets to live.

Maria has trouble seeing the boundary between freedom and forgetfulness. She may use money to boost her mood—without noticing where it actually hurts.

They both struggle not just with financial choices, but with the pressure of who they think they ought to be.

But there is a way forward—and as we've seen repeatedly, it begins with self-awareness. When we understand why we do what we do, we can start finding solutions that work for us—not against us.

Exercise: Who Are You in Financial Disguise?

We've now been introduced to five economic personality types: the Planner, the Bon Vivant, the Minimalist, the Protector, and the Freedom Lover.

This exercise invites you to explore where you fit in—not to put you in a box, but to give you a mirror you can adjust and nuance with both curiosity and humor.

1. Who do you most resemble?

Read through the five types again and then ask yourself:

- Which type do you instinctively feel closest to—without over-thinking it?
- Which type would you rather not resemble (and why)?
- Is there a type you only recognize in yourself during specific situations—like when you're stressed, happy, or in love?

2. How do you view your own type?

This is about self-insight with a touch of humor. Try to answer honestly—and a little kindly:

- What's the best part about being "me" financially?
- What's the most impractical part?
- What do others often say about the way I handle money?
- What nickname would my banker give me?

3. The type I keep in my back pocket

Some sides of us only show up when we allow ourselves to play.

- If I could freely try out another type, which one would it be?
- What do I think I could learn from that type?
- What might be hard about trying it out?

4. My Financial Alter Ego

End with a playful statement like this:

"I'm a ____ at heart, but I have a hidden ____ in my gut.
When I spend money, I'm trying to achieve ____.
And if I dared to be curious, maybe I could try ____."

Example:
"I'm a Planner at heart, but I have a hidden Bon Vivant in my gut.
When I spend money, I'm trying to achieve safety and control.
And if I dared to be curious, maybe I could try buying something without knowing exactly why—just because it feels good."

The purpose of the exercise isn't to change you.
It's to meet yourself with warmth and recognition.
Because behind every financial strategy lives a person.
And that person—you're getting to know a little better now.

Closing: When We Dare to Take Our Finances Personally

Talking about financial personality types might sound silly. But sometimes, in the silly lies the truth.

When we can laugh at how we approach money, we open the door to something more honest—and more loving.

You're a person trying to find your balance:
Between control and freedom.
Between safety and enjoyment.
Between planning and impulse.

The goal isn't to get it "right"—but to become aware.
And maybe to discover that behind the type you usually identify with,

there's a small, quiet voice ready to join you the next time you reach for your card.

It starts with knowing who you are.
And with daring to smile at it.

Chapter Summary

Financial Personalities and the Language of Love

In this chapter, we explored how our financial behavior not only reflects our spending habits but also reveals our emotional structures, needs, and defense mechanisms.

We met a range of financial personality types and saw how they can clash—or complement—in close relationships.

We looked at how money is often used as an emotional language—especially in love:

We engage in comfort spending, withhold, give gifts, or hide purchases—not just for financial reasons, but to protect ourselves, seek connection, or regulate emotions.

We explored typical patterns and how money—often unconsciously—becomes a way to communicate vulnerability, needs, and boundaries.

We were reminded that true financial intimacy requires courage, trust, and vulnerability—and that only then can we start to "speak the same language."

The chapter ended with an exercise inviting humorous and compassionate self-awareness:

Who am I when I spend money?
Which parts of me show up—and which ones do I keep hidden?
Because in the end, money isn't just about numbers.
It's about people, stories—and the courage to face ourselves.

Chapter 10

WHEN DREAMS BECOME DOMAINS

When Longing Takes Shape

In this chapter, we'll look at a variation of the theme 'making conscious choices.' We return to the idea of finances across different domains, and explore how we can consciously prioritize dreams by assigning them a domain.

Dreams as Images and Longings

Dreams have a way of taking form. They rarely appear as pure emotions, but rather as images:

A summer cottage in Sweden.
A sailboat in the evening sun.
A small shop with coffee and books.
A world without alarms, emails, and Excel sheets.

We don't just dream of moods—we dream of things, places, and scenarios. That makes sense. The body and mind need something tangible to navigate by.

But sometimes the form becomes so strong that we forget what it was we were really longing for.

We chase the boat, the house, the café—and perhaps only realize too late that it wasn't what we truly needed. It was what we thought it would give us.

Jonas had a boat dream

He saw himself on the deck with the wind in his hair and no plans in his calendar.

He started researching prices, marina spots, and maintenance.

But the closer he got to the dream as a concrete project, the more it began to tighten around his shoulders.

Something didn't feel right.

Not because the dream was wrong—but because he hadn't tuned into what he was actually seeking.

In this chapter, we'll explore just that:

How dreams become economic choices—and how we can make them thoughtfully.

We'll look at how to separate form from longing. And how to—maybe for the first time—give your dreams a place in your finances, without letting them take over everything.

Maybe it's not about fulfilling the dream. Maybe it's about *finding its core—and living from that place.*

When Dreams Are Mistaken for Solutions

There's a particular kind of dream that sneaks in during walks, sleepless nights—or in encounters with others' apparent freedom.

The dream of something different. Something bigger. Something more true.

But in our eagerness to understand and act, we usually give the dream a form. It might turn into one of the following thoughts:

"I want to buy a house in the countryside."
"I want to start my own business."
"I want to take a year off and travel."

And right there lies a great risk—that we're mistaken. Not because the dream is wrong—but because we believe the form is the answer.

That what we long for can be wrapped in bricks, boat engines, or plane tickets.

But a dream is rarely a solution.
It's a signal. A language our inner self uses to say:

"I miss something."
"I long for something else."
"I want to feel myself."

When we turn the dream into a solution—without listening to what it's trying to say—we risk building something beautiful that doesn't fit us.

We get the house, but not the peace.

We get the freedom, but carry restlessness with us.

That's why the next step doesn't begin with another calculation—but with a question:

"What feeling am I really longing for?"

Only when we know that can we find forms that take the longing seriously—instead of hiding it.

From Feeling to Action — A Five-Step Model

When you ask a company what it wants to create, you rarely begin with products. You start with the feeling or the vision.

In the same way, we can work with our personal dreams—not as finished plans, but as sources of something deeper: a feeling, a value, a life in motion.

Here is a simple five-step model you can use when a dream is calling to be heard:

Feeling — what do I want to feel?

Start with the inner world.

Forget the boat, the house, the sabbatical for a moment and ask:

How do I imagine I'll feel when the dream becomes real?

Is it freedom?
Silence?
Meaning?
To be closer to something real?
Or simply: less pressure, more space?

The feeling is the nerve of the dream—and it deserves to be felt before we run after the forms.

Value — what does it mean to me?

Ask yourself:

Why is this feeling important to me?

Maybe it's about reclaiming something you've lost. Maybe it points to a part of you that you miss. Or maybe it's a longing for something you've never allowed yourself to take seriously.

When you know the value behind the feeling, the dream becomes not just something you want—but something you want to honor, to give room to.

Possible Forms — what could it look like?

Only now should you begin to look at the form—but do it broadly, freely, and playfully.

In what possible ways could this feeling take physical shape?
What does it require—and what might it not require at all?

Example:
You long for immersion. That could be:

— A writing retreat
— A regular morning without a phone
— A membership at a studio
— A notebook and a closed door every Sunday

The form doesn't have to be dramatic to be true.

Economic Domain — where does it belong?

Once you've found possible forms, then ask:
Which economic domain does this belong to in my life?

— Is it an investment?
— Something that requires saving up?

— Something that can fit into my existing finances?

— Something I can test on a small scale?

Placing the dream in the budget doesn't make it less poetic—it makes it possible.

First Action — what do I do now?

Finally:

What is one small step that brings me closer to the feeling? Not to the entire dream—but to what it holds.

— Maybe you take a walk in silence and sense whether the calm already lives inside you.

— Maybe you call and sign up for an introductory course.

— Maybe you sit down with a piece of paper and write:

"If I truly listened to myself, I would…"

Small steps count—especially when they point toward something big.

This model is not a recipe.

It's a language.

A language that makes it possible to speak with your dreams—and listen to what they're truly saying.

Jonas's Boat Dream — and What He Was Really Seeking

Jonas had had the same dream for several years:

He wanted a boat.

Not a luxury yacht, just a small sailboat. One that could sit in the harbor, ready for weekends filled with freedom, saltwater in his hair, and unplanned quiet.

He pictured himself in a windbreaker and cap, coffee in hand and waves beneath him.

A man with time. Peace. A space of his own.

He started researching the market.

Hours flew by on classified sites and YouTube videos about maintenance, sail types, and marina fees.

He made spreadsheets with different scenarios: buying new, buying used, sharing with a friend, selling again in five years.

But the more concrete it became, the less right it felt.

Something began to tighten. Not just in his stomach, but in the dream itself.

Something didn't fit.

He sat down and asked himself:

"What is it I'm really picturing when I imagine being on that boat?"

He grabbed paper and pencil—not to write numbers, but feelings:

— "I picture freedom."
— "Silence. No emails."
— "Being alone—in a good way."
— "Going away without asking anyone."
— "Owning something that doesn't make demands."

And then it dawned on him:

It wasn't the boat he longed for.

It was a feeling. Something intangible—that might be found in other ways.

He began thinking in new forms:

— Renting a boat for two weeks a year instead of owning one.

— Going alone to the coast with a thermos and blanket every Sunday.

— Buying a journal and writing one page a week about what freedom means to him—and how he practices it.

And something changed:

The dream of the boat didn't disappear.

But it became free.

It became a possibility—not a necessity.

And Jonas felt he had taken a step toward something real.

Not toward the boat. But toward himself.

Maria — Investing in Something That Can't Be Bought

Maria didn't have one big dream. Not a boat. Not a shop. Not a country house. But she had a feeling that kept coming back.

It was like a small longing that surfaced in quiet moments—a mood she had almost forgotten. Something about being absorbed, immersed, a little lost in her own world.

It wasn't on any wish list. But she knew how it felt.

She had felt it as a child, drawing for hours without any sense of time or goal.

She began searching online:

Drawing classes, watercolor weekends, creative retreats.

But everything seemed either too expensive, too ambitious—or too foreign.

And she recognized something familiar:

She was in the process of turning something inner into something outer.

Something quiet into a project.

So she sat down and asked herself:

"What is it I'm really longing for?"

The answer didn't come immediately, but it was clear:

"I just want permission to be creative—without goals and without performance."

She went out and bought a notebook and a box of colored pencils. Nothing expensive. Nothing special. But something that could lie on the table and call to her.

She set aside two hours every Wednesday evening.

Not as an obligation—but as an opening.

The first evening felt strange.

She didn't really draw anything. Just doodled. Made odd circles and strange shapes.

But she stayed. And that was what made the difference.

Not the result—but the space.

After a few weeks, she began looking forward to it. Not to create something beautiful.

But to meet herself in that space.

She discovered that the mood she had longed for had already begun to return.

Not through a big investment. But through a small, conscious choice:

To take her longing seriously—in a way that fit her life.

What Are *You* Really Longing For?

Maybe you also have a dream of a boat.

Not necessarily with mast and sail—but as a symbol of something you dream of. Something you imagine will change your life. Give you peace, freedom, joy, or meaning.

Maybe your boat is a new kitchen.
A year at folk high school.
Quitting your job.
Starting over.
Or something much smaller—but with a big feeling behind it.

Try for a moment to take a step back. Not to give up your dream. But to listen to it more precisely.

What is it you're really longing to feel?
What mood or experience hides in your dream?
Is it freedom? Immersion? Feeling at home in yourself?

And what other ways could that feeling take shape in your life?

Is there a small action, a new rhythm, a decision—that could already now bring you closer to what you're hoping for?

Dreams aren't just for those with surplus and good finances. They belong to all of us. But to carry them with dignity, we must be willing to listen curiously—and act with care.

You don't have to wait until you can afford something big. You can start small. Because what you long for rarely lives in the boat itself—but in you.

When a Dream Becomes an Economic Domain

There is a special power in discovering what you're truly longing for. When a dream is stripped of its outer forms and you're left with the mood itself—freedom, immersion, peace, presence—you're closer to something real.

It's a wonderful feeling that truly affirms your integrity.

The next step is just as important:
How do I make room for it?
Not just in my mind—but in my everyday life and in my finances?

For many, dreams end as frustrated longings or impulsive actions. Either we never get started—or we throw ourselves into something without direction.

Both leave us unsettled.

That's why this section isn't about limiting dreams—
but about carrying them with responsibility and structure.
Finding a way for them to live, without taking over everything.
Giving them a real place in our finances.

Imagine your finances as a landscape with different areas:
Housing. Food. Transportation. Savings.
But why not also an area for what makes life feel alive?

A Domain for Your Dreams

Not as something you have to apologize for—but as something you choose to take seriously.

When a dream gets its own domain, two things often happen:
It becomes more real—and therefore more possible.
It loses its destructive power—because now it is met, not denied.

It's not about making everything add up. But about showing yourself that your longings are welcome. Even in the spreadsheet.

What Is an Economic Domain? (a brief recap)

An economic domain isn't just a budget line.

It's a way of recognizing that money also carries meaning.

That our lives have areas where we spend—and choose—with our hearts.

Most people already have several domains, even if they've never called them that: A food budget. A retirement savings. An account for vacations or gifts. Areas in the finances with their own purpose and rhythm. And often their own emotional weight.

When we place something in a domain, we're saying:

"This matters."

We don't have to decide again and again—because the frame is set. And we can do the same with our dreams.

When a dream gets its own domain—a defined place in our economic life—it's no longer a vague longing or an impulsive temptation. It becomes part of the whole.

A dream in a domain is no longer an either-or question.

Not something we have to give up—or throw ourselves into headfirst.

It gets a seat at the table. It becomes part of the conversation, not something that secretly throws off the balance.

It can be as simple as a small account in your online banking with a name that means something to you.

A budget line marked "My Freedom."

A fixed rhythm in your calendar, where you allow yourself to be creative or slow or present—depending on your dream's color.

The point isn't to make the dream economic.

But to give it a form where it can breathe and grow—without being forgotten or repressed.

Different Types of Dream Domains

Not all dreams are the same. Some feel essential to life. Others are like faint echoes of something we can't quite hear yet. Some can be realized now. Others require time, courage, and preparation.

To navigate with respect and care, it helps to ask:
What kind of dream am I holding—and how should it be carried?

Here are three types of economic dream domains that can help you find form and direction:

Life Investments — Dreams with Depth and Direction

Some dreams reach into the core of who we are—or want to be.
They're about identity, meaning, and life direction.
These might be dreams of changing your life, switching paths, or setting new priorities.

Examples:
— Taking a sabbatical to write, travel, or care for a sick parent.
— Pursuing further education or learning something new.
— Moving out of the city and establishing a new way of life.
— Spending less money and living more simply.

These dreams often require planning, financial awareness, and patience. But if they get their own domain—with a name, a space, and a rhythm—they become not just possible, but more present.

A life investment domain could be:
— A dedicated account
— A personal five-year plan
— A yearly wheel with milestones and breaks
— A monthly reflection on where you are in relation to the dream

Quality-of-Life Enhancements — Dreams Nourished in Daily Life

Not all dreams require upheaval. Some are about making the life you already have feel more like yours. Creating pockets of joy, presence, immersion, or freedom within your everyday.

Examples:
— A regular hour to paint, write, or read.
— A monthly budget for small outings.
— A subscription you truly enjoy.
— A work-from-home day that starts with a walk.

Here, it's not about saving or restructuring. It's about conscious permission.

You tell yourself: "This matters, even if it's not essential."

This domain becomes your own reminder that small things also deserve space and respect.

Exploration Domains — Dreams in Testing

Some dreams we don't yet know what to do with.

They're exciting, but also uncertain.

They call to us, but we're unsure whether they're real, possible, or even ours.

Examples:
— A thought of moving to another country.
— A budding interest in a new field.
— An idea to start something on your own.
— A desire to live with less—but without being ready yet.

An exploration domain is about giving yourself permission to be curious. Without obligation—but with respect.

It could be:

— A monthly "dream hour" for research and reflection

— A small amount set aside for experiments

— A conversation with someone living what you're considering

— A notebook with one question: What do I want to know before I decide?

Giving your dreams a domain—regardless of type—makes them human.

They are allowed to live in the space between the possible and the dreamed.

Not as demands. Not as illusions. But as guiding stars. And that brings both freedom and peace.

How Do You Make Room for a Dream in Your Budget?

There's something special about seeing a dream get its own place in your budget.

It's like planting a seed—not in the ground, but in your trust that something good will grow. And it's not as complicated as it may sound.

The first step is to take the dream seriously.

Not as a luxury problem, but as part of the life you want to live.

You don't ask: "Can I afford it?"

But: *"How can I give it a good beginning?"*

Here are a few simple approaches:

Create an account with a name that means something to you.

Maybe you call it "My Freedom," "Dream Account," or "Something Important."

The name makes a difference. It helps you remember what it's about.

When you transfer money—even small amounts—it feels meaningful.

You're not just saving. You're choosing yourself.

Make it visible in your budget.

Many people have fixed categories for rent, food, and transport.

But what about a fixed category for what makes life feel alive?

It could be $25 a month. Or more. Or less.

What matters is that it has a place—not in your surplus, but in your structure.

Use rhythms, not just amounts.

Maybe your dream isn't financially heavy—but requires time and attention.

So create a rhythm. A regular evening each week. A weekend every month. A day each quarter.

Your calendar can be just as important as your online bank.

Some dreams grow best in time, not money.

Start small—but begin.

You don't have to wait until you have clarity, surplus, or a big plan.

You can start with one decision. One hour. One transfer. One thought you take seriously.

When you give the dream a home in your finances, something subtle but powerful happens:

It's no longer just something you hope for—but something you act on.

And that creates a new sense of self-respect.

When Finances Becomes a Matter of Self-Respect

Some think finances is about numbers, priorities, and self-discipline. And it is. But beneath the surface, it's often about something deeper:

Self-respect.

How we relate to money often reveals how we relate to ourselves.

Do we allow ourselves to take up space?

To want something?

To say no to what drains—and yes to what nourishes?

When we give our dreams a place in our finances, it doesn't just affect the money—it changes us.

We begin to feel:

"I am worth taking seriously."

"My needs count—even the quiet ones."

"It's okay for me to choose what's good for me."

Self-respect in finances isn't about pride or consumption.

It's about making choices aligned with what matters.

About saying: "This is my life. I choose to spend my resources on what has value for me."

Even if it's invisible to others.

That can be hard in a world where money is often tied to status, performance, and comparison.

But that's exactly why it matters so much.

A person with economic self-respect doesn't need to justify their choices.

Doesn't need to explain why something is important.

Because they feel it.

And act accordingly.

When dreams and finances are allowed to meet in respect, a new language emerges in life.

A language where you're no longer subject to your finances—but in dialogue with it.

More Space Without More Money

Sometimes we think we lack money—but in reality, we may just need a new perspective on what we already have.

In working with economic dreams, it can help to explore which parts of our finances have become invisible to us. These are expenses, habits, and items we no longer question—because they feel so natural. But these areas often hold untapped potential.

Housing is a good example. Maybe we live where we've always lived—without realizing that just a few kilometers away, the financial picture could be completely different.

The vacation home, the car, the subscriptions—things that once mattered deeply, but could now be reimagined.

You might be able to rent out your home a few weeks a year—and cover a significant portion of your costs.

Maybe you could manage with one car instead of two.

Maybe you could switch mobile providers or cancel a service you barely use.

All this might sound very practical. But at its core, it's about freedom.

About daring to ask:

"Is this still something I choose—or something I've just landed in?"

If we dare revisit the obvious, we open up to new possibilities—not necessarily by *cutting back*, but by *restructuring*.

It's not about reducing your quality of life—but about bringing it closer to what you truly long for.

You might call it *value-based optimization*—bringing your finances more in line with the life you want, by renegotiating unconscious habits.

Dreams need space. And sometimes that space is hiding where we least expect it—in the things we've stopped noticing.

Exercise: *What Is Actually Up for Negotiation?*

This exercise is about looking at your finances with fresh eyes.

Not to cut back—but to discover where freedom might be hiding.

1. Write down three financial areas you never question.

Examples: housing, car, subscriptions, leisure, food, gifts, savings, vacation, tech, clothing.

2. Choose one area and ask yourself:

— When did I last consciously choose this?

— What do I actually get from it?

— Has something in my life changed that affects my needs?

— Are there other ways to approach this that would give me more space—without costing me something essential?

— What could I prioritize instead if I freed up some resources here?

3. Write a sentence that begins with:

"It surprises me that I might actually be able to ..." or *"I've never considered that maybe I don't need ..."*

This exercise isn't about cutting everything away—but about re-choosing with open eyes.

From Jonas's Boat to Maria's Studio — Two Examples

When we talk about dreams and economic domains, it can easily sound abstract. But let's return to Jonas and Maria.

Because in their stories, we see how dreams can come to life—with direction—without being postponed or overdone.

When Jonas realized that it wasn't necessarily the boat he longed for—but the feeling of freedom, calm, and personal space—something shifted.

Instead of going into debt or letting the dream fade away, he found a new solution: A small economic domain with room for what he missed.

He created an account called "Freedom on the Water." Not with the goal of buying a boat right away, but as a way to keep his longing alive and tangible.

He deposited $100 each month—not as an obligation, but as a conversation with himself. A reminder that his dream mattered.

At the same time, he started taking solo trips to the water. And when the opportunity arose, he rented a boat for a day.

The dream became real—not in its original form, but in its spirit.

Maria didn't have a grand plan. But she had a longing to be creative, without goals or performance. And she knew that if she did nothing, that longing would fade again.

So she created a framework.

Not a studio or an expensive course—but a corner of the dining table. She bought a small box of colors and a sketchbook. And she carved out time: two hours every Wednesday evening. Not because she had to achieve something—but because it was valuable to be present in her own creative process.

She also created a small line in her budget: "Creative Joy —$30/month." Money she could use on supplies, paper, paints—or just a café where she could sit and draw.

It wasn't the amount that made the difference. It was the fact that her creativity had a place.

Both examples show how dreams can live—when they're allowed to take a shape that fits the life you're already living.

Dreams as Beacons — Even When They Don't Materialize

Not all dreams come true. Some remain ideas, sketches, fantasies. And that's not necessarily a problem. Because dreams serve a purpose, even when they're not fulfilled. They point. They show what matters. They help us understand who we are and where we long to go—even if the path remains inaccessible.

A dream can function as a beacon, even if we never reach it.

Like a star on the horizon we adjust our course by, without expecting to touch it.

Jonas didn't buy his own boat.

But his longing for freedom made him prioritize differently.

He said no to certain tasks.

He began working more flexibly.

He discovered that freedom lived less in the ship—and more in how he organized his life.

Maria didn't become an artist.

But her studio—and the hours she set aside—gave her a new sense of self-connection.

She began seeing her creativity as a resource, not something she had to defend.

When we meet a dream, we don't have to ask: How do I fulfill it?

We can instead ask: What is this dream trying to show me?

Because maybe it's not about making the dream come true.

Maybe it's about letting it become true within us.

Living With Your Dreams — Not Chasing Them

There is freedom in discovering that dreams don't have to be destinations.

They can be dialogues. Invitations. Questions we get to live with—and answer in small steps, in our own words.

When we dare to look beyond the form and find the core of the longing, we can begin to live with our dreams—without letting them control us.

And when we give them space in our finances—not necessarily a big space, but a real one—something happens to the balance in our lives.

We begin to sense the difference between what is necessary and what is meaningful. And we understand that our finances is not just a framework for consumption—but a way to honor what we dream of.

Reflection Questions

What dream have you carried with you for a long time—without doing anything about it?

If you look beyond the form, what feeling do you think the dream is trying to give you?

What is the value behind that feeling—and why is it important to you?

What small forms could that dream take in your current life—without turning everything upside down?

How could you give the dream space in your finances? Through money, time, attention?

A Small Exercise

Draw a circle on a piece of paper.

Write "My Dream" in the center.

Draw five branches from the center and label them:

— Feeling

— Value

— Possible Forms

— Economic Domain

— First Action

Spend 10 minutes on each branch.
Write down whatever comes up—without judging.
Just listen.
Let it be the beginning of a conversation.
Between you and your dream.
Between your finances and the life you want to live.

Chapter 11

QUALITY OR QUANTITY?

How to make wise financial decisions by knowing your purpose and starting from within.

When we face the choice – quality or quantity?

You've likely been there. You're standing between two options—maybe a new job, an apartment, a vacation, a new phone, or a hobby. One promises more: more for your money, more features, more possibilities. The other may seem simpler—but also more thoughtful, more authentic.

This is where the choice between quality and quantity begins to stir.

It's a decision that rarely has to do with money alone. It's about how you want to live your life. What you prioritize. And what you truly need—not just in your finances, but in your relationships, your time, your energy, and your self-respect.

In today's world, quantity often gets the spotlight. More clicks, more friends, more projects, more activity, more stuff. We live in a culture where 'more'easily becomes a synonym for 'better.'

But that's precisely why this kind of decision calls for a pause. A small step back. To ask yourself a simple but important question:

What is it that I really want?

Is it abundance that brings me peace—or depth? Is it variety that enriches me—or immersion?

This chapter isn't about glorifying one over the other. It's about recognizing what you truly want. What fits the domain you're in. And how, by seeing yourself a little more clearly, you can make choices that leave you feeling more satisfied.

Putting on the 'domain lens'

In this book, we've explored the idea of economic domains—that life isn't one big economy, but many small spaces with different goals and values. When you look at the quality-versus-quantity question through the lens of domain thinking, the question shifts. It's no longer: *What's best in general?* But instead: *What matters here—in this specific domain?*

In some domains, quantity makes a lot of sense. You might be aiming to gain experience, explore something new, expand your reach, test ideas, or simply get things moving. In these cases, it's not crucial that every part is perfect—what matters is that you act. That you make progress, take initiative, ship things, and get seen. For example, when you're writing content for social media, practicing a new language, or selling low-margin products—here, quantity might be what moves you forward.

But in other domains, it's exactly the opposite. Here, quantity can muddy the waters, create noise, and distract from what truly matters. In your close relationships, your value-driven projects, or in what you create to bring deeper meaning into the world—it may be quality, focus, and presence that bring fulfillment. Here, it's not about how much you do—but how you do it.

That's why it's so important to know your *purpose* before choosing your strategy. And this is where domain thinking helps. It reminds us that our lives shouldn't be measured by the same standard across the board. You can be quality-focused in one area and productive in another—as long as it aligns with your values and goals.

A personal example: When quality becomes quality of life

I've personally reached a point in life where quantity is no longer the most important metric. As a retiree, I don't need to secure a high income or compete with others. What I *do* need is to create something that feels meaningful. Something shaped by the life I've lived—and what I hope to pass on.

For me, this has involved writing books. Not because I need to make a living from them. Not because I expect them to become bestsellers. But because the process of writing—gathering thoughts, experiences, and insights—is deeply satisfying. It brings order to my inner life. It gives me a sense of coherence. And it lets me offer something that might resonate with or help others.

When I finish a book, I feel that I've given something real. Something of value. And that brings a quiet joy. If others read it, that's a gift—especially if it's someone I care about or feel connected to. But the meaning of the work doesn't lie in the number of readers. It lies in the *quality* of what I've shaped. And in what I've gained from doing it.

Still, I feel the constant lure of quantity. I could write more books, publish more, be more visible. And it often feels like that's what I *should* do. That it's the broader path, the faster path, the more visible path. But if I follow that impulse uncritically, I risk losing what matters most: depth, grounding, quality—and with that, the connection to what makes it meaningful to me.

That's why I need to ask myself: *What was my starting point? What truly gives me satisfaction?*

And the answer is rarely 'doing more.' More often, it's 'doing what matters—with care.'

When I Sold Pancakes on the Street

When I had just retired, I found myself with a sense of both freedom and emptiness. I had chosen to leave the job market—not because I was no longer able to work, but because I wanted to give myself the chance to choose something new. It was important to me that my third age became a time where I defined my own direction—not just a phase of drifting quietly into stillness.

While I waited for an idea to appear, I started stopping by a small mobile coffee cart on my daily walk. It was run by a young man in his late twenties who had just returned from a long journey in the East. He had an openness and curiosity that was contagious. We quickly got into the habit of chatting—over coffee, about psychology, philosophy, life choices. For me, it became a highlight of the day, a small oasis of meaning.

One day he said, half-jokingly, "Henrik, shouldn't you be selling something too?" And that sparked something in me. Not long after, I began selling pancakes from a little cart. Later, I switched to coffee, and eventually we actually started a business together. We had fun, met countless people, and spoke with all kinds of passersby. It was a social experiment, a life project, and it gave me exactly what I had been missing: presence, connection, and a meaningful platform in daily life. Quality, at my own pace.

But our situations were very different. I didn't need income—I needed meaning. He, on the other hand, was building a life with a family and needed daily revenue. For him, good conversations and cups of coffee weren't enough. There had to be money in the till. And I completely understood that.

Our business grew, and within a year we had multiple carts, some converted bikes and vans, and were being hired for corporate events and private parties. Suddenly we could earn in one afternoon what used to take us days on the street. It became more professional, more efficient, more about quantity. But for me, it also became less meaningful.

I noticed my enthusiasm waning. What had carried the project—the spontaneity, the human connection, the open encounters on the street—was disappearing. And I realized I had betrayed my own starting point. I had said yes to something that made sense in *his* domain—but not in mine. That was an important realization. Because what, for him, was a budding livelihood had, for me, become an empty workday.

We parted as friends. He took over the business, and I stepped away. Because my goal was never to scale or optimize—it was to live.

The Little Avocado Grove

Today, I live in Argentina, and my main occupation is growing avocado plants and trees. I spend hours in my greenhouse and on the land—not because I need to make a living from it, but because it brings me a quiet joy. And when people hear about my project, they almost always ask the same question: *"What will you do when they start bearing fruit?"* How will you sell them? What about production? Logistics? Their perspective is often economic, and I understand that—many of them are in the middle of working life and need their projects to yield a return.

But I can feel that I'm once again in a different domain. It was never my ambition to become an avocado farmer in the traditional sense. What I dreamed of was a small avocado grove—maybe 100 trees—where I knew each individual one. I wanted to graft them myself, follow their growth, tend to them, and find the right spots in the soil where they would thrive. It wasn't the idea of yield, but of *connection*, that carried the project.

And in the beginning, that's exactly what it was. I started with 50 plants and felt rich. But without really noticing, the number began to grow. I took cuttings, planted new ones, experimented. And suddenly one day, I was standing in my greenhouse with 500 plants. That might sound like a success story—but it wasn't, not quite. Because slowly, it began to change my perspective. I started thinking in terms of land area, labor, and expenses. I needed more land. I had to get help. And the joy began to fade.

In the end, it was actually a frost that reminded me where I had started. An unusually cold winter night killed 90% of my plants. I was left with 25–30 surviving trees. And that was when, as I sat in my chair looking out at them, I felt a strange sense of relief. Because now it was possible again: to follow them one by one, to remember their grafts, their placements, their temperaments. To be present in the *small*, instead of drowning in the *big*.

I was reminded that it's through close attention that joy grows. When I walk outside and see that one tree carries a branch from another variety I grafted—and it's thriving—that gives me a completely different sense of satisfaction than if I had harvested 200 more kilos. Maybe I won't use the fruit for export, but for guacamole in my pancakes when I'm selling them at the market. It may not be efficient, but it's *right* for me.

This is an example of how quantity can trick us into thinking we're growing—when in reality, we may be moving away from what we hoped to find. And how quality sometimes requires a loss to return.

The Paradox of Choice – More Isn't Always Better

The American psychologist **Barry Schwartz** has, in his book *The Paradox of Choice – Why More Is Less*, put words to a feeling many of us know all too well: we become exhausted by having to choose. Not because we lack options—but because we have too many.

In a modern world overflowing with choices—from dozens of types of milk in the supermarket to life paths and retirement plans—we might assume that more freedom leads to more happiness. But Schwartz points in the opposite direction. When we are presented with too many options, we become uncertain. We start to analyze, compare, and wonder what we might be missing, no matter what we choose. The result is often not greater satisfaction—but less. And perhaps most importantly: a growing sense of doubt in ourselves and our decisions.

Schwartz distinguishes between two types of people:

- *Maximizers* – those who always strive for the best possible outcome and therefore constantly analyze, compare, and optimize.
- *Satisficers* – those who look for something that's 'good enough,' and find it easier to feel content.

When we pursue quantity—more products, more projects, more growth—we risk ending up as Maximizers: trapped in a constant search for what we don't yet have. And we never feel quite satisfied. But when we choose to limit ourselves—to pick fewer things, with more awareness—something else happens. We invest more presence into what we've chosen. And we discover that enough can actually feel like enough.

In my own experiences—with avocado trees or the mobile coffee business—I could clearly feel how more began to cloud my focus. The problem wasn't the choice to sell coffee or to grow trees—it was the sheer number of options, investments, and future scenarios that began to steal the joy. It was only when something was stripped away—by life or by my own hand—that I could again feel a sense of simple satisfaction.

The paradox of choice isn't just about consumer goods. It's about life decisions. About how many doors we should really try to keep open—and when it's wise to say yes and no with a peaceful mind.

Søren Kierkegaard: The Existential Choice

When we speak about conscious choices and quality of life, it's hard—especially for me as a Dane—not to mention the philosopher Søren Kierkegaard. His thoughts on existence, choice, and responsibility laid the foundation for what we now call existentialism.

For Kierkegaard, personal choice wasn't just about practical decisions—but about existence itself. It is through our choices that we become who we are—and that is why choosing is so profoundly serious. Not because we must always choose *correctly*, but because our choices shape our lives and our sense of self.

He describes different stages of life. The '*Philistine*' lives unreflectively—following the crowd, adapting to norms, habits, and convenience. In this stage, quantity often becomes the default logic: accumulating, buying, working, optimizing—without stopping to ask why.

The *'Aesthete'* lives more consciously, in search of beauty and pleasure—perhaps even quality—but often without taking full responsibility. Choice becomes a game where the aim is to feel alive, not necessarily committed.

The *'Ethical'* person, by contrast, embraces life choices as something deeply personal and accountable. Here, it's no longer about what brings pleasure or what others admire—but about what is *right*, and in tune with one's own inner voice.

Kierkegaard's point is that we only become ourselves through self-chosen commitments. And this is where his philosophy meets the question of quality versus quantity. Because it is precisely when we pause and ask: *What truly matters to me? What feels true?*—that we make choices that strengthen our integrity.

I've felt many times how the logic of quantity has pulled me in one direction—while my own inner voice whispered something else. And every time I've chosen to listen and act consciously, it has made a difference. Not just in the *content* of my life—but in my experience of being truly alive.

When Quantity Becomes a Necessity

It might sound as if I always choose quality over quantity. But that wouldn't be true. Because I've also seen how a quantitative mindset can be necessary—yes, even vital—if what you're passionate about is to become more than just a hobby.

Shortly after I left the workforce, I joined an entrepreneurship course. We were a mixed group of people—different ages, different life situations—but we all shared a desire to create something of our own. Some had concrete projects, others just had a sense—a dream that hadn't yet taken shape.

It quickly struck me how many of the participants had gone through something meaningful in their lives that they wanted to pass on. There were artisans, therapists, small-scale entrepreneurs—all carrying a passion, a craft, an insight. There was something beautiful about it: the quality in their thinking, the personal engagement, the authenticity in their work.

But again and again, it became clear how hard it was for them to turn their ideas into a livelihood.

It was as if quality and quantity couldn't coexist. Most of them had never thought in terms like production, scaling, marketing, or pricing. Many feared that "selling" their product would dilute it—make it less pure, less real. They were afraid of losing what had brought the idea to life in the first place.

But reality was relentless: if they wanted to make a living from it, they had to find a way to scale—without losing their soul in the process. One stunning ceramic bowl or one inspiring session wasn't enough. They had to find a rhythm, a structure, an economic sustainability. Here, quantity wasn't just a strategy—it was a necessity.

This was an important lesson for me as well. Because sometimes we can romanticize the small, the handcrafted, the intimate—so much so that we lose sight of how something can actually be brought into the world and make a difference for others. Quantity isn't necessarily emptiness. Sometimes, it's precisely what allows a quality value to be shared.

Finding Your Own Balance

Looking back at the various examples from my life, it becomes clear to me that the question of quality versus quantity can't be answered in black and white. It's not about one always being better than the other. It's about knowing yourself. And daring to ask: What is my starting point? What is my goal? What are my limitations?

Sometimes things grow—like my avocado plants—without me ever intending them to. Other times, you need to intentionally turn up the quantity—like my young coffee cart partner, or the participants at the entrepreneur course who had to find a way to live off their passion. It's not wrong, as long as it aligns with what you want. But it requires vigilance. Because it's easy to get carried away—either by the urge to expand and grow, or by the ideal of staying close to the unique and personal.

Domain thinking reminds us that we don't need to judge ourselves by someone else's goals. If *my* domain is life quality and meaningful everyday experiences, then that's where I should look for my compass. If *your* domain is financial independence or spreading an idea, that's where you need to find your balance. It's only when we dare to look clearly at our own starting point that we can truly choose—not just between less and more, but between what is right for others and what is right for *me.*

Quality and quantity are not opposites. They are compasses. And we can use both—but only if we're the ones holding the map.

Reflection Exercise: *What Is Your Starting Point?*

Think of an area in your life where you often face the choice between quality and quantity. It might be your purchases, your work, your hobbies, your relationships—or something else entirely.

Answer these questions for yourself:

1. What is my goal in this area—what do I want to achieve or experience?
2. What are my current limitations? (time, money, energy, life situation)
3. When does it make most sense for me to choose quality—and when quantity?
4. Is there a place where I've compromised my original intentions?
5. What could I adjust if I wanted to return to my own sense of balance?

Tip: Try drawing a scale from 1 to 10, where 1 is pure quality and 10 is pure quantity. Mark where you are right now—and where you'd like to be.

Chapter 12

INHERITANCE, GIFTS, AND THE SACRED MONEY

Why Some Money Feels Heavier Than Others

Money with Baggage

Maria sat alone at the dining table. In front of her lay the purple envelope. It had been there for two days, since she got back from visiting her mother. She hadn't opened it yet. Not because she didn't know what was inside—but because she knew all too well.

"Just a little love gift," her mother had said with a warm smile as she pushed the envelope across the table. "You need a little breathing room in your finances."

Maria had smiled back. Politely. Gratefully. But inside, the familiar knot was growing.

It wasn't the first time. And every time, the feeling crept in: That the money wasn't just a gift, but also a reminder. That she hadn't managed on her own. That her mother still, somehow, was holding her up.

She inhaled and opened the envelope with a finger under the flap.

Bills. $1000.

Maria laid them on the table. Stared at them for a moment. Then she got up and put on some coffee—as if she could postpone the decision a little longer.

It wasn't the amount that was the problem. It was what it represented.

How do you use money that feels… complicated?

Not because it's dirty. But because it carries a story. A tone. A meaning you didn't choose yourself.

She knew she ought to be happy. But she felt—like so many times before—a little less free.

Reflection — When Money Isn't Just Money

It might sound spoiled.

To sit with $1000 and not know what to do with it. But it's not that simple. Because money is rarely just money.

They are stories.

They are relationships.

They are remnants of conversations we never finished.

They come with feelings, glances, silences, and expectations.

That's why some money feels heavier than others. Not in the hand—but in the body.

Some money lands like freedom. Others like a burden.

And the difference rarely lies in the amount. It lies in where the money comes from—and what it brings with it.

When Maria looks at the check from her mother, she doesn't just see $1.000.

She sees a concerned look.

Old conversations about how one 'ought' to do things.

The feeling of once again being the one who receives—not the one who stands on her own two feet.

We each have our own versions:

— An inheritance from someone we had a complicated relationship with.

— A money gift we didn't ask for.

— A compensation for an experience we'd rather forget.

— Or just money that lands in our lives in a way we don't quite know how to accept.

Some money feels untouchable.

Others like an invitation.

And some like a test: Will you now do the right thing with it?

Mental Accounting — When We Create Inner Accounts

Maria was still staring at the check. It was money—yes. But it wasn't just money.

It was money from a specific person. Given in a specific relationship. At a specific time. And therefore, it didn't land on the same shelf as salary, savings, or the grocery budget.

It had gotten its own mental space.

And right here, behavioral economist **Richard Thaler**'s concept of mental accounting becomes a key.

He showed how we humans unconsciously divide our finances into small mental 'accounts.'

Not one overall budget—but many little pockets, each with its own rules and feelings.

We have vacation money. Food money. Emergency funds.

And then there are those we don't talk about:

Gift money. Inheritance money. 'Black' money. Guilt money.

Money we don't just spend—but feel our way through.

Thaler explained that this mental division helps us navigate a complex reality.

When we sense the difference between 'fun money' and 'responsible money,' we gain structure and direction.

We can plan, protect ourselves—and sometimes stay true to our values.

But… it also comes at a cost.

When the accounts become too rigid, the money becomes inflexible.

We freeze it. Give it rules we don't dare to break.

And sometimes we end up feeling trapped—not by the amount, but by the meaning.

Think again of Maria.

If she had won $1000 in the lottery, she might have spent them spontaneously. If she had earned them at work, they'd go straight into the budget. But because they came from her mother, they went into a different account. An account we might call: mother-money. And mother-money follows different rules. You don't just spend it. You're supposed to use it 'wisely.' Or maybe not at all.

They come with a kind of unspoken etiquette:

"You may accept it—but don't forget where it came from."

When the Rules Get in the Way

Thaler says it clearly: Mental accounting isn't irrational. It's a way of bringing order to Quality or Quantity?

that might otherwise feel overwhelming. It's a kind of psychological ledger.

But if we never take a closer look at which accounts we've set up—and who actually wrote the rules—then we risk sitting with money we don't dare to touch. Not because we can't. But because they mean too much. Or too little. Or something entirely different than we thought.

Gifts — Invisible Invoices and Emotional Ties

Jonas had expected it to be just another Tuesday.

He was tidying up in the kitchen when he heard the soft ping from his phone. A message from Rune, his old university friend:

"Check your email. A little gift — just because."

Jonas smiled. That sounded like Rune. Spontaneous, generous, a bit unruly.

He opened his email—and saw a travel agency gift card. $200.

In the 'personal note' field, handwritten:

"For an experience — because you need it."

Jonas sat down.

First came the joy. The warmth.

It felt like a kind of financial hug—an unexpected love letter in numbers and possibilities.

But almost as quickly, something else crept in: a small unease.

Nothing major—just a sting.

Because… why now?

And what was he supposed to do now? Write a long thank-you? Invite Rune out? Return the gesture in some way?

He could feel how his mind was already keeping a kind of invisible score—even though Rune had written "just because."

Something unsaid hung in the air.

A balance that might have shifted.

And that made the gift feel less light—and more complex.

Jonas got up and walked around with his coffee cup.

The gift card was still open on the screen.

He wanted to use it. But something held him back. Not because he wasn't grateful. And not because he didn't appreciate Rune.

It was just… hard to place.

It was as if the gift card didn't belong on any of the shelves he usually sorted financial decisions into.

It wasn't a salary, a bill, an investment, or savings.

It was just… something else.

Here we can turn to **Mary Douglas**' ideas on cultural order and symbolic weight.

Douglas, an anthropologist and systems thinker, wrote about how we—as societies and individuals—organize the world into categories: *pure and impure, permitted and forbidden, everyday* and *sacred.*

When something doesn't fit into the known categories, we don't know where to put it.

Then it becomes sacred.

Or dangerous.

Or… immovable.

That's exactly what Jonas experienced.

The gift card from Rune wasn't just a gift. It was a gesture that didn't fit. And precisely for that reason, it came to a standstill—not physically, but mentally.

According to Douglas, it's not the object itself that causes discomfort—it's the lack of placement.

That goes for gifts too.

An heirloom from a distant relative.

An envelope of money from an ex.

A gift from a boss you have a complicated relationship with.

If we don't know where to place it—in which box, what meaning, what language—it lingers.

Like an open question we don't know how to answer.

Jonas was still staring at his screen.

Maybe it wasn't the gift that was heavy.

Maybe it was the missing language that made it unbearable.

He needed a ritual. A framework. A way to make the gift his own.

Not just financially—but emotionally. A way to shift it from undefined to usable.

Even though Jonas hadn't yet used the gift card, it had already triggered something inside him.

An inner unease. A desire to reciprocate. Almost like a reflex.

And this is exactly where **Marcel Mauss**' classic theory from the 1920s becomes helpful.

Mauss showed that gifts are never neutral.

Even when we call them free, loving, unconditional—there's often something that comes with them.

Not necessarily a demand. But a relational expectation.

A gift, he said, isn't just a thing. It's an act that creates a connection.

And connections… come with obligations.

When we receive something—consciously or not—an imbalance is created. And we feel that we must give something back. Not necessarily the same. Not the same amount. Not right away. But something. A sign. A gesture. An acknowledgment.

Mauss called it "the invisible contract."

And that's exactly what Jonas feels.

He knows Rune doesn't expect anything. But he also knows that something within himself does.

Not out of compulsion—but out of bond.

And that's what makes it complex:

The invisible invoice isn't sent by the giver.

It's written by the receiver—with emotions as ink and conscience as paper.

You may have experienced it yourself:

Receiving a gift that felt 'too big'—and suddenly feeling small.

Getting a gesture you couldn't return—and feeling guilty.

Saying "thank you"—but feeling it wasn't enough.

Or giving something you hoped would bring joy—but instead created distance.

This is when the gift stops being a gift—and starts becoming an imbalance.

And what happens then?

Well, we try to close the balance.

By giving something back.

By downplaying our joy.

Or—in some cases—by not using the gift at all.

We put it away. Let it sit.

Not because we're ungrateful—but because we can't carry its meaning.

Jonas had put the gift card in a drawer.

But the thoughts kept returning.

Should I invite Rune out?

Should I send him something?

Or just say thank you more clearly?

He knew Rune didn't expect anything.

But he also knew he expected something of himself.

And maybe that's exactly where the invoice was written.

When the Gift Becomes Sacred

Some gifts can't simply be used.

Not because they're too valuable in money—but because they mean too much.

They are charged.

With *history*. With *emotion*. With *symbolism*.

It could be an heirloom from a deceased grandmother.

A note with handwriting.

A money gift with subtext.

A check from an ex.

A photo.

A letter.

An object that never found a proper place.

We place them on a shelf. Let them lie in a drawer.

We don't touch them—not because we don't want to, but because we can't.

We don't know how to accept them—without violating something.

Something human. Something relational. Something sacred.

Here **Mary Douglas'** theory becomes relevant again.

She writes that societies (and people) organize their world by separating the 'ordinary' from the 'sacred.'

The sacred is what we don't treat like everything else. What we don't move. Don't trade. Don't mix into everyday flow. It has its own sphere.

And in daily life, we experience the same:
A piece of jewelry we're afraid to wear.
A sum of money we can't bring ourselves to touch.
A gift we dare not regift—but also can't use.

The gift is no longer just a gift.
It has become a symbol.

Examples of sacred gifts:

A woman receives her grandmother's ring. She dares neither to wear it nor sell it—and she can barely admit that she doesn't actually like it.

A man inherits a painting that reminds him of his father's death. It hangs in the living room, but he never looks at it.

A daughter receives a transfer from her mother with the message: "In case I'm no longer here…"

The money remains untouched for years.

Reclaiming the Gift — Without Giving It Back

Making a gift your own takes courage.
It requires you to ask:
What does this gift mean to me?
Is there something unspoken I need to acknowledge?
And how can I receive it—without feeling bound?

Maybe the gift needs to be passed on.
Maybe it needs to be used—as an act, not just a function.
Maybe you need to say aloud what it stirs—and thereby set it free.

Because a gift that can't be used is no longer a gift.
It has become an obligation without purpose.

But the moment we take responsibility for the meaning—and put our own words to it—the gift can come alive again.

It can once again become... a gift.

Maria and Jonas — Two Gift Stories

Maria had never had a close relationship with her boss. They exchanged polite greetings. Shared small talk by the coffee machine. But their contact was marked by distance and efficiency.

That's why she was surprised when, just before Christmas, she was handed a gift card.

"Thanks for your effort," the boss had written. "You really work hard."

The gift card was for $150 toward an exclusive spa stay.

Maria smiled and said thank you. But inside, she felt something else.

Because yes, she had been busy. Really busy. She'd worked extra shifts, been flexible—but also felt pressured, invisible, a bit worn down.

And now came a gift card. Not a conversation. Not spoken recognition. Just a gesture.

It began to feel as if the gift card was meant to close something she actually needed to open.

A band-aid instead of a meeting.

A kindness that also shut something down.

So she put the card in a drawer—and couldn't bring herself to use it or throw it away.

Jonas experienced something different.

He had recently mentioned to his sister that he was working on a small startup project. Just in passing. Nothing big. No expectations.

But a few weeks later, a MobilePay transfer arrived: $250 With the note: "For your dream. No questions—just cheering from here."

Jonas was touched.

But right after came the unease:

What if it didn't work out? Would she follow up? Would he disappoint her?

Was it freedom—or a responsibility?

The money remained in the account.

Not as a reserve, but as a reminder.

An unspoken obligation. An expectation he wasn't sure he could fulfill.

It wasn't the amount.

It was the fact that she had seen him. Believed in him. And set something in motion that he now had to carry forward.

Both situations show how gifts are never neutral.

They are social actions. They create movement—but can also create imbalance.

They touch our sense of worth, our need for freedom, our fear of being in debt.

Sometimes the gift becomes a bridge.

Other times a boundary.

And sometimes it takes a new gesture—for us to free ourselves again.

How to Receive—Without Getting Trapped

Receiving a gift should be simple.

A warm gesture. An opportunity for joy. A connection.

But for many of us, it's connected to something deeper.

Something that touches old patterns:

— Guilt.

— Need for balance.
— Fear of being indebted.
— Uncertainty about what the gift really means.

We have—often without realizing it—learned that gifts come with strings.

That we owe something in return.

That there's a bill, even when no one says it out loud.

So we smile. Say thank you. Maybe tuck the gift away. Not because we're ungrateful, but because we don't know how to receive it without losing a bit of ourselves in the process.

But what if we could practice a different way of thinking?

Not as naive receivers who ignore the complexity.

But as people who dare to explore it—and find new ways forward.

Reflection: Why Is It Difficult?

Try asking yourself a few questions—without looking for the right answer:

What do I feel when I receive something I didn't ask for?

Can I say "thank you"—without also feeling I owe something?

When was the last time I gave something hoping to be seen or acknowledged?

When was the last time I received something I couldn't bring myself to use?

It's not about judging—but about understanding.

Because gifts carry meaning. And we can become better at clarifying that meaning—both when we give and when we receive.

The Language of the Gift — A Small Thought Tool

Imagine that every gift—whether physical, financial, or symbolic—has its own key signature.

A language that speaks between people.

A language we often sense, but rarely name.

Some gifts say:

Care: "I see you. I know you need this."

Recognition: "I'm grateful for what you do."

Freedom: "You can use this however you want."

Expectation: "I hope this leads to something."

Repair: "This is my way of saying sorry."

Control: "I want to have influence."

Attachment: "I want to be closer to you."

By asking yourself:

"What language does this gift speak?"

you may begin to hear something you've previously overlooked.

And by asking:

"What language do I want to speak when I give something?"

you can begin to give with greater clarity—and fewer hidden contracts.

Because the gift lies not only in what is given—but in how it's given.

And the clearer we become in our gift-language, the freer both giver and receiver become.

Being able to receive something—without immediately needing to reciprocate—is a form of freedom.

It takes courage. And trust. Courage to stand in the open. Trust in the relationship. And in yourself.

And the same goes for giving.

To dare to give without strings. Without invisible expectations.

To be able to say: "It was my pleasure." — and mean it.

When we open up to the language the gift truly speaks,
it can become something different than we imagined:
A movement instead of a bind.
A relational invitation instead of a hidden contract.
A gesture in freedom instead of a bill to be paid.

We can begin to give and receive with greater clarity.

See what's really happening between us—behind envelopes, gift cards, and small MobilePay transfers.

And when we see it, we can also begin to set ourselves free.

Not necessarily from the money—but from the unspoken, the heavy, the binding meaning inside it.

Chapter Summary: When Money Carries Meaning

In this chapter, we've seen how money isn't always neutral.

Some money comes with baggage.

They aren't just amounts—they are relationships, feelings, expectations.

We've met Maria, who receives money from her mother and feels she's also receiving an old role she thought she'd left behind.

We've seen how Jonas gets a gift and immediately begins balancing gratitude with guilt.

We've learned from Richard Thaler that we mentally place money in different "accounts"—and that some accounts are almost untouchable.

We've seen through Mary Douglas how things without a clear place become "sacred"—and therefore hard to handle.

And we've understood with Marcel Mauss that gifts almost always come with an invisible contract—a social obligation to give back.

But most importantly:

We've gained language to talk about the unspoken.

To recognize when money creates movement—and when it creates bonds.

And we've gained perspective that it's not the gift itself, but the way we receive it, that determines whether we become free—or trapped.

Chapter 13

WHEN FINANCES HAVE COLLAPSED

When Everything is a Mess — and You Don't Know Where to Start

Many have watched TV programs where a family in financial crisis gets help from a professional advisor. Often, it starts with a huge shock: bills that haven't been opened for months, consumer loans spiraling out of control, and a bank statement that looks like a tragedy in numbers. The viewer is left with a mix of sympathy and bewilderment. *How could it get so bad?*

But I have mixed feelings about those programs. On one hand, they highlight something important: that financial chaos isn't just about ignorance—but often about fear, shame, and loss of control. On the other hand, the solution is often presented in very black-and-white terms: a strict advisor imposes a rigid budget where the family can only spend $50 a week on all 'unnecessary' items. There's often no room for missteps, no room for care, no room for being human.

This might give the viewer the impression that there is a clear path out—if you just *pull yourself together*. But for someone in crisis, it can feel intimidating. Because what if you can't live by an Excel sheet without exceptions? What if it's that very pressure that caused everything to fall apart in the first place?

When Self-Respect is More Important than Self-Realization

When finances have derailed and unopened envelopes are piling up, there is almost always a heavy feeling underneath: shame. Not just about what has happened—but about what one fears it says about them as a person. The shame can be so intense that it's no longer about numbers, but about identity. About failure.

That's why it's so difficult to help someone who is in the middle of chaos. It can be tempting—for both the person themselves and those around them—to think: 'You need to get a grip. You need to realize what's going on.' But that's exactly when you risk adding even more shame—and pushing the person even further from a solution.

Perhaps in those cases, we need to do something a little different from what we've suggested earlier in this book. Maybe you shouldn't start by drawing connections between financial behavior and psychological patterns. Maybe you shouldn't begin by analyzing what went wrong. For many, in that situation, it would only feel like another judgment. Another failure.

Maybe instead, you should try—gently—to separate the finances from the person. Not because there isn't a connection. But because self-respect needs to be strengthened before one has the courage to face reality.

Because even in the worst financial breakdowns, there are often good intentions behind them: the desire to manage on one's own. The desire to protect others. The desire to hold on to an identity where you're not the one who fails. Or simply the strength it takes to hold everyday life together—while the envelopes pile up.

And within those intentions lies the beginning of something important: a core of will, care, or responsibility that can become the foundation for the next steps. It's not about avoiding responsibility—but about finding a way to take responsibility without losing yourself in the process.

So if you're the one sitting with finances in ruins: Don't start by fixing yourself. Start by finding something you can respect in yourself. Something you would respect if it were a friend in the same situation.

It might be the courage to even read these lines. It might be the desire to make things better. It might be that you've held something important together—while the finances crumbled. This is not to absolve you of responsibility. It's to give you the strength to take it.

Fighting with What You Have

When finances have collapsed, it's like any other crisis in life: the longer it's been going on, the harder it can be to find a way back. Not because it's impossible. But because the energy has been spent on maintaining appearances—or keeping fear at bay.

That's why it's important to understand: This is not just about money. It's about crisis management.

And as with any crisis, it's crucial that we don't just look at the *problem*—but also at *ourselves*. Who am I when I'm down? What has carried me through tough times before? What are my natural reactions, and what strengths do they hold?

Some gain energy by talking to others. Others need silence to feel themselves.

Some need structure and plans. Others need hope and dreams.

Some are strong in the practical. Others in the emotional.

Some can ask for help. Others hold on—alone.

There is no single right way.

But there is one important movement: To *mobilize* what you have.

Because even if it feels like you've lost your overview—you haven't lost your experience. The person you are now contains everything you've learned before. Everything you've overcome before. It's still there. You just need to find your way back to it.

And when it succeeds—when you begin to see yourself as *a person in a financial crisis*, rather than *a failure with a ruined finances*—something happens. It doesn't create solutions in itself. But it builds strength. And strength is exactly what's needed to begin taking action.

I believe in the gentle path. Where you don't start by being corrected—but by being heard. Where the goal is not perfection, but stability. And where the budget is not a prison—but a tool to take yourself seriously again.

Crisis management is also psychological

When you begin to catch your breath and the acute part of the crisis starts to subside, it can be tempting to just leave it all behind. Just move on. On with life. On with the plans. But precisely at the point where things begin to brighten, it's important not to skip the most crucial part: understanding.

Because it's not enough to survive a financial crisis. The question is: *How did you survive it?* What carried you through? What aspects of yourself did you have to activate? And which ones might have been set aside?

What we choose to carry forward becomes our foundation. And if that foundation consists only of emergency tactics, escape, or over-responsibility, we risk building on something that might collapse again later.

So at some point, in the aftermath of the crisis, you must pause and ask:

What did I learn about myself?

What was my strength during this time?

And where are my vulnerable spots—the ones I might not have noticed before?

We all have experience with crises. We've all handled something before—which means we have resources we can draw on again. But many of them are overshadowed by shame, guilt, and exhaustion. That's why an essential part of the work is to reconnect with the sides of yourself that *can handle things*. Not to shut out the pain—but to find your footing within it.

Creating a new inner collaboration

There's a reason things fell apart. For some, it's external: unemployment, illness, divorce. For others, it's more about inner patterns—and for most of us, a mix of both.

When rebuilding your finances—not just in dollars and cents, but in *psychological strength*—it's essential to look at which inner forces were at play.

We're not made of just one voice. We consist of several sides—characters, impulses, ways of being in the world.

Some people have a strong, forward-driving side. One that sets goals, brings ideas to life, takes chances. But maybe that side pushed another away—a more cautious and reflective side trying to remind you of limits, responsibility, and balance.

Example: One part of you burns for new projects, while another watches the bank account and pulls the brake—both have something important to say.

It's not about choosing one over the other. It's about getting them to *talk to each other.*

You might call it an inner collaboration:

That the strong one leads—but is accompanied.

That the cautious one speaks up—but doesn't paralyze.

That the vulnerable one isn't hidden away—but is listened to.

That the responsible one doesn't run the show alone—but gets support.

It might sound abstract. But in practice, it's about recognizing that we contain multiple sides—and that true change begins when we allow all of them a seat at the table.

So ask yourself:

Which two (or more) characters live inside me?

What does each one need?

What would happen if they collaborated—instead of clashing?

Many financial problems start as inner conflicts. And many financial solutions therefore require inner integration.

Chapter 14

WHEN LOVE AND MONEY MEET

Daring to Bring Differences Into the Light

Money is never just money in the realm of love

It often starts with something small.

A bill at a café. A gift that feels too big. A comment that lingers in the air.

A glance that changes the mood. A silence that says more than words.

Two people sit across from each other. Maybe they're in love. Maybe they've known each other for years.

But the moment the question arises — "Should we split it?" — something happens.

Something invisible, yet palpable.

Suddenly, it's no longer just about coffee or concert tickets.

It's about status. Independence. Care. Dependency.

It's about vulnerability.

Because in the space of love, money is never just money.

We may think we're discussing budgets or payment methods.

But often, we're really discussing safety.

Or control.

Or the unspoken contract we carry from childhood or past relationships.

One person feels ignored when the other spends impulsively.

The other feels surveilled when asked about expenses.

One feels pressured when the other wants joint finances.

One feels alone when money is never discussed.

Money doesn't just serve a purpose — it becomes a mirror.

It reflects where we feel inadequate.

Where we long for something else.

Where we try to protect ourselves from rejection, dependence, or shame.

This is where **Vicki Robin** becomes an important voice. In her book *Your Money or Your Life*, she describes money as a relational practice:

"The way we use our money reveals our true values — not just as individuals, but as a society."

Robin emphasizes that money always expresses more than mere buying and selling. It shows what we value. What we choose to spend our life energy on. When we share finances with another person, we don't just share money — we also exchange life values, priorities, and experiences. This makes money a sensitive area where misunderstandings easily arise.

Brené Brown, a researcher in vulnerability and courage, adds a crucial perspective:

"What we don't talk about holds power over us."

And this is especially true for money — and especially in love.

Because here we have the most to lose. Not financially, but emotionally.

Brown emphasizes that vulnerability is not weakness, but courage: the courage to show up honestly without any guarantee of being met. When we avoid talking about money in a relationship, it's often due to fear of being misunderstood or rejected. But that very silence can create distance.

That's why we stumble when love and money meet.

We've rarely learned to talk about money — and certainly not with an open heart.

But before we can navigate shared finances, we must understand where each of us comes from.

Our Financial History — and How It Stays With Us

We all come from somewhere.

And that includes our relationship with money.

Some of us grew up with abundance. There was always enough, but money was rarely discussed—how it was earned or why it was spent the way it was.

Others grew up with scarcity—or a *sense* of scarcity, even when there was technically enough.

Some were taught that money was private—something you didn't ask about.

Others saw money used as reward, punishment, or covert power.

For some, money was linked with security—for others, with shame.

These patterns follow us.

Not always visibly, but like an invisible script.

Like a filter in front of our eyes—shaping how we make decisions and try to understand others' choices.

Maybe you've experienced it yourself:

— Feeling guilty when you spend money on something that brings you joy.

— Feeling 'wrong' even when you can afford it.

— Struggling to ask for financial support because you were taught to handle things on your own.

Our financial history is like a backpack we carry into every relationship.

It's filled with experiences, stories, shadows, and treasures.

And it's with us—whether we're aware of it or not.

That's why two people in a relationship rarely speak the same financial language.

One grew up believing money should be saved, hidden, and used with caution.

The other learned that money is meant to bring joy, freedom, and spontaneous opportunities.

One finds comfort in budgets and planning.

The other feels suffocated by control and spreadsheets.

There's no right or wrong.

But there *are* differences—and they often don't show up until you live closely together.

Vicki Robin writes that our relationship with money is shaped by our "financial socialization"—the process through which we learn what money means, who has it, and what it's supposed to be used for.

It's a social and psychological legacy we carry. And it's only when we become aware of that legacy that we can begin to act freely.

Brené Brown adds an important psychological insight:

"People don't act from bad intentions—they act from protection."

When two financial histories collide, there's often friction—not because one wants to hurt the other, but because both are trying to protect something vulnerable.

That's why financial understanding in love doesn't begin with a joint account or a shared budget—

It begins with a shared question:

"Where do you come from—financially speaking?"

When we dare to ask that question—and truly listen to the answer—we can begin to understand not just each other, but ourselves in a new way.

When the Differences Become Visible

You can understand each other's stories *in theory.*

You can nod, listen with openness, and feel enriched by the conversation.

But it's only when the differences show up in everyday life that the real work begins.

It's rarely the big decisions that cause conflict.

It's the small things.

The repeated frictions.

Moments when values meet—or collide.

When silence becomes heavier than words, and a single action can feel like an attack, even if it wasn't meant that way.

This is where we meet Jonas—looking back.

A relationship that began with warmth and curiosity, but where financial differences gradually became a source of distance and misunderstanding.

Jonas and His Ex — Two Currencies in One Relationship

It started well.

She was spontaneous, lively, and a little chaotic — exactly what Jonas was craving at the time.

He was calm, grounded, and a bit reserved — and something in her seemed drawn to that.

They balanced each other — at first.

But after about six months, Jonas began to notice something.

It wasn't about big amounts. It was about vibes.

She bought gifts for no reason. Paid for lunches he hadn't asked for.

And then there was the trip.

They had planned a long weekend in Berlin.

Jonas, true to his nature, had made a spreadsheet.

Not to limit her, but to make sure they both felt secure.

He had broken down the expenses: transport, accommodation, food, experiences.

But already on the first day, she started improvising.

She wanted to eat at new restaurants every day.

Bought two tickets to a show without asking.

Suggested shopping, even though they had agreed to keep costs low.

At first, Jonas felt it as a sense of unease.

Then irritation.

Eventually distance.

They talked about it. But not very well.

She said:

"You're so controlling. I feel suffocated."

He replied:
"You don't respect our agreements. I feel invisible."

But they didn't talk about what it was really about.
Her fear of being held down.
His fear of losing his footing.

Jonas still thinks about it sometimes.
Not because he regrets the breakup.
But because he now understands that the money stood for something more.
Something they never put into words.
He hid his vulnerability behind structure.
She hid her longing for freedom behind spontaneity.

Today, Jonas is more curious.
Not about the spreadsheet — but about what lies behind it.

Maria and the Younger Man — Money as Both Resource and Taboo

It wasn't something Maria thought much about when they first started seeing each other.
Yes, he was younger — but not inexperienced.
He was kind, curious, quick-witted, and easy to be around.
And he looked at her with a mix of admiration and genuine interest, something she hadn't felt in a long time.

They talked about music, movies, old books, and strange questions about life.
When they laughed together, the age difference felt like a footnote.

She enjoyed it. She enjoyed him.

She was well aware that her financial situation was different from his.

She had a stable job, had inherited a small apartment a few years earlier, and now had the kind of financial freedom she had worked hard to build.

He was in the middle of his third freelance phase and was temporarily staying with a friend.

But that didn't bother her. In fact, she found it a bit freeing.

He seemed uninterested in status and performance, and it felt easy to be in his company.

Still, she started to notice small shifts.

The first sign was so subtle she almost ignored it.

They had planned to have dinner together on a Friday.

She suggested a cozy café.

He smiled, but suggested instead a walk and maybe a cup of coffee.

She said yes without hesitation.

But when it happened again a few weeks later — another gentle refusal of an invitation — she started to wonder.

Especially when she noticed the hesitation every time the bill came.

He would say kindly, "I'll get the next one." But the next one never came.

A small doubt began to creep in.

Was there something they weren't saying?

Maria decided to take the lead.

She didn't want ambiguity and misunderstandings to trip up something that otherwise felt good.

The next time they met, she suggested a restaurant and said with a light smile:

"I really want to treat today. It just feels like that kind of Friday, doesn't it?"

He hesitated for a moment, but thanked her.

His expression was hard to read — relief? Embarrassment?

She let it go and kept the mood light.

But Something Had Shifted

He was quieter that evening.

His gaze drifted more often.

And when she later suggested a small getaway to a nearby coastal town, he quickly replied:

"That sounds lovely, but I think I need to take it a bit easy financially right now."

Maria nodded and said she understood.

But inside, she felt a pang.

An imbalance she hadn't seen coming.

It wasn't about the money.

It was about what wasn't being said.

About what she suddenly wasn't sure she was allowed to bring into the relationship.

She began to feel… wrong.

Not because she had said something wrong.

Not because she had too much.

But because her financial freedom now felt like something that had to be hidden.

Something that maybe created distance—instead of closeness.

And it surprised her.

Because she had never seen her finances as a burden.

On the contrary—it was something she had built herself.

Something she was proud of.

But now it felt like an invisible wall.

Something that couldn't be spoken aloud without making everything awkward.

Maria's Reflection — and Facing Her Own Vulnerability

When she got home that evening, Maria sat down on the couch without turning anything on.

No music, no TV.

Just silence and a cup of tea slowly going cold in her hands.

There was no conflict to replay, no disagreement to analyze.

Still, the feeling lingered in her body: a distance, hard to put into words.

Something had shifted—and it unsettled her.

She began replaying the past few weeks in her mind.

How many times she had initiated plans.

How she had wrapped her suggestions in innocent phrases:

"I happened to get paid a bit early."

"I was actually planning to eat out alone—want to join me?"

It dawned on her that she had—almost imperceptibly—started hiding something.

That she was ashamed of something she had once been proud of:

Feeling secure.

Having built her own financial freedom.

Being able to treat someone without worrying afterward.

And then the question crept in:

When had it become taboo to be strong?

She went quiet inside.

When had she started hiding her freedom to avoid making someone uncomfortable?

When had she learned that strength could feel like a threat?

She remembered a podcast she had recently listened to.

Brené Brown was talking about vulnerability—and said something that had stuck with her:

"Vulnerability isn't about showing where we are weak—it's about daring to show what we most protect. What we're most afraid to lose."

Maria Robin back a little.

It was as if the words struck a nerve.

Maybe it wasn't about his finances.

Maybe it was about her own fear of being misunderstood.

She realized that in her eagerness to keep things light, she had started to tone herself down.

That she had pulled back her freedom—not to create balance, but to avoid standing out.

It wasn't him who had asked her to do that.

It was her own idea of what could create connection—and her fear of what might break it.

But in smoothing out the differences,
something honest had also disappeared.

She thought:

Maybe it's not about compensating.

Maybe it's about inviting.

Not with a gift or a dinner—but with words.

With conversation.

With the courage to say:

"This is me. Not to make you feel small.
Not to take up more space—but to share who I am."

The Hidden Systems — How Money Regulates Emotions

As human beings, we've always found ways to soothe anxiety and enhance joy.

We seek balance, relief, connection.

And we use what we have at hand.

For some, it's food.

For others, words.

For many—perhaps more than we think—it's money.

This becomes especially clear in romantic relationships.

When life is intense, emotions are strong, and words don't always suffice,

we often start to regulate the emotional climate using the most available tool: finances.

We pay for dinner without saying why.

We buy a gift instead of offering an apology.

We withdraw from shared expenses as a silent protest.

We hold back—or spend impulsively—not because it makes sense,

but because it brings peace in the moment.

It's not a sign of weakness.

It's a human instinct.

But precisely because it's so human, it's also easy to overlook.

We say it's "just about the money"—but it rarely is.

Especially not between two people who love each other,

each carrying invisible needs and old patterns.

Typical Patterns in Emotional Regulation Through Money

When we don't quite know what we feel—or don't dare say it out loud—we often start to act.

And in many relationships, we act with money.

It's not because we're superficial.
On the contrary.
It's because money is a discreet way of expressing something we don't always have the words for.

Here are some of the most common patterns:

Spending as Comfort

"I've had a tough week—I deserve this."

A new pair of shoes, dinner out, a weekend getaway.
It feels like a gift to oneself—and maybe it is.
But sometimes, the comfort purchase covers something else:
A feeling of inadequacy, of being alone, of not being seen.
When the partner questions it, it doesn't feel like curiosity—but like criticism.
Because it wasn't just about the money.
It was about relief.

Frugality as Control

"If I don't keep track of every penny, I lose myself."

Some find safety in knowing every expense, every receipt, every scenario.
But it can also become a shield.
A way to keep chaos and emotions out.
The partner may feel there's no room for generosity or spontaneity—but it's not about stinginess.
It's about holding oneself together.

Gifts as Declarations of Love

"I show you I love you by paying for you."

Gifts can be touching and meaningful.

But they can also be the only way someone has learned to express love.

When the recipient doesn't react as expected, it can feel like rejection.

And then the giver withdraws—without words.

Because it wasn't just a gift. It was a declaration.

Secret Spending as Freedom

"I need to have something that's just mine."

When everything in daily life feels shared, the longing for autonomy can grow.

A hidden subscription. An account the other doesn't know about.

Not out of disloyalty—but as a breathing space.

But secrets create distance, and distance breeds mistrust.

These patterns are rarely conscious.

But they are powerful.

And they shape the way we live together.

Money as Communication in Relationships

Most couples talk about money.

But only a few realize that they're constantly speaking with money—and often without words.

Money becomes part of the emotional language.

We send signals, show care, set boundaries—all through financial actions.

A paid meal can be a declaration of love.

Or an apology.

Or an attempt to take control.

Rejecting a gift can be self-protection—but may also be perceived as coldness.

A secret purchase might be a cry for freedom—but feel like betrayal.

When we lack a language for our feelings,

we begin to use money as a substitute.

And like with any language:

"If we don't understand each other's codes, misunderstandings arise."

That's why it's important to become aware of how we 'speak money'—and what we're really trying to say.

When Emotions Rule the Ledger — A Psychological Reflection

We often believe that finances are rational.

But in reality, they're driven by emotion.

We act from the gut, the heart, from past experience—not from spreadsheets.

And when emotions take the wheel, we suddenly follow completely different logics.

We spend to feel worthy.

We deny ourselves to feel moral.

We hide because we don't dare to ask.

We spend because we don't dare to feel.

Money becomes a mirror—and what we see isn't always pretty.

But it's honest.

When emotions take control, we lose not just our overview—

we also lose connection.
To ourselves. To each other.

True financial change begins with courage.
The courage to say:
"I don't know why I'm doing this."
"It feels wrong, but I don't know how to change it."
"This isn't just about money—it's about me."

Small Scenes from Real Life

The Gift That Went Unnoticed

She had spent days finding something special.
He said "thanks" — and put it away.
She got angry.
Not about the gift.
But about not being seen.

The Offer That Covered Up Shame

He said the backpack was on sale.
It wasn't.
He wanted something nice — but didn't dare own it.
He had grown up believing you only bought what you "needed."

The Home Without Money Talk

They never talked about money.
But the air was often tense.
Behind the conflicts lay something unspoken.
A sense of unfairness.
They didn't talk about money — but they lived inside it.

What They All Had in Common:

It wasn't about the amount.

It was about feelings, connections, and vulnerabilities.

And only when those were acknowledged could anything begin to heal.

Financial Trust and Open Conversations

Money is sensitive.

It takes courage to talk about it.

When we open up about money in a relationship, we're not just sharing numbers.

We're sharing stories, fears, longings, and shame.

Trust must be built.

Slowly. Honestly.

It's not about agreeing — it's about being able to show up without being rejected.

Trust doesn't happen when everything is perfect.

Trust happens when we stay in the conversation — even when it's hard.

Exercise: Financial Self-Portrait and Loving Exchange

This exercise is a game — an invitation to closeness and curiosity.

Part 1: Your Financial Self-Portrait

Write down your answers — separately, without talking first:

My financial childhood in one word and one object: ________

When I have money in my hands, I most want to…

The most unreasonable thing I've bought (that I love):

If my financial personality were a dog:

Something I rarely say about money but wish I could:

Part 2: Exchange Portraits

Read your answers aloud to each other. Listen, laugh, and ask with curiosity.

Bonus Round: Loving Currency

Invent a non-financial gift for each other:

A walk in silence. A lunchbox with a note. A conversation without interruptions.

Something that costs nothing — but counts.

Closing: When We Dare to Count on Each Other

Money isn't the most important thing in love.

But it plays along — like undertones and shadows.

When we dare to look at it together, we also dare to see each other more clearly.

We discover that we count differently.

But we can still count on each other.

Chapter 15

THE ECONOMIC ECOSYSTEM

Joint Lecture — Two Voices, Two Perspectives

The room was neutral—almost too neutral. White walls without decorations, gray stackable chairs arranged in straight rows, and a table with water bottles and thin paper cups. On the screen at the front of the room, blue text read: "Economic Awareness and Life Choices — a Conversation about Values, Rhythm, and Responsibility." No speakers, no stage lights—just the clear sound of plastic bottles being opened and jackets being draped over chair backs.

It was a weekday evening, and the participants trickled in slowly, wearing all kinds of expressions. Some looked curious, others more skeptical. A woman whispered to her neighbor that she hoped it wouldn't be too dry. An elderly man took a seat in the front row and carefully laid out a notepad and pen. The room had no real atmosphere yet—as if it were waiting to be filled with something. With presence. Or meaning.

Everything was practical and impersonal—as if the place itself had chosen not to take sides. For that very reason, everything said in there was heard with a special clarity. As if the bare walls offered a kind of pure resonance.

Jonas stepped into the room with a slight hesitation. He had seen the lecture listed on the library's website a few days earlier and had immediately felt a strange impulse to sign up. Not because he was really uncertain about his finances—he paid his bills, had some savings, and kept his spreadsheets. But still. Something had been gnawing at him lately. A feeling that he might be staring too hard at the numbers without understanding the map itself.

He found a seat in the middle of the room, neither at the front nor the back. He draped his jacket over the chair and pulled a notebook from his bag. The pen clicked softly between his fingers, as if he were already preparing for something. Not necessarily answers—but maybe new questions.

He looked around. People of all ages, many with the same searching look in their eyes. He wasn't alone. There were others here who looked like they hoped for a little push. A shift in direction. A new way of seeing something they thought they already knew.

Jonas folded his arms—not in resistance, but in reflection. He was here. Not entirely voluntarily, perhaps. But not forced, either. Maybe something inside him had insisted on taking this evening seriously—without him knowing why.

Maria entered a bit later than most. She slipped in with a quiet, apologetic gesture, as if she would rather slide in unnoticed. She chose a seat at the back, close to the wall, where she could see everything without being seen herself. That was how she felt most present—a little at a distance, but fully awake.

She hadn't told anyone she was going to a lecture about money. It sounded far too grown-up, far too dry. But in reality, it had sparked a tingling curiosity in her. Not because she lacked control—quite the opposite. She had always had a good overview of her spending, her accounts, her goals. And yet, lately, she had felt trapped in her own reason. As if something was missing—some rhythm, some balance, something she couldn't find in her spreadsheets.

She had written a sentence in her calendar when she signed up: "Maybe it's not about money. Maybe it's about me." She had almost laughed at herself afterward. But now she was here. With that sentence glowing in the back of her mind.

From her seat, she could see the speaker setting up, and in a brief glance, she let her eyes sweep the room. She didn't notice Jonas, but her gaze rested for a moment on the middle row. She didn't feel alone.

There was something in the air. A hint that this might not be just an ordinary evening. Not a solution—but maybe a beginning.

Money is stories

The speaker stepped forward in front of the screen. She was middle-aged, dressed in a navy-blue jumpsuit, and her gray hair was tied in a bun that radiated both simplicity and experience—as if she were both a professional and a poet. She didn't begin with numbers. She began with a sentence that immediately changed the atmosphere in the room:

"Money isn't just money. Money is stories we tell ourselves—and each other."

An almost imperceptible pause followed. Several in the audience shifted slightly in their seats. Jonas perked up. Maria stopped fiddling with her pen.

"We think we control our finances with budgets and strategies," the speaker continued, "but maybe it's actually our finances that control our life choices, our relationships, our hopes—and our fears."

Jonas felt a tremor behind his ribs. He wrote the word *fear* in the margin of his notebook and drew a circle around it. Fear? That wasn't something he normally associated with money. But maybe... maybe it wasn't entirely wrong. Maybe it was fear that always spoke first when he considered changing something in his life.

Maria sat up straighter. She had expected a dry presentation on investment or debt structures. But this was something else. When the speaker described money as relational voices—something we both hide behind and reach out with—Maria felt struck. She had always been good at organizing and managing. But she had never thought about what her way of handling money actually said about her. About her need for control. Her way of asking for space.

A new slide appeared on the screen:

Economic Ecology: When Our Choices Are Interconnected with Others

Jonas leaned forward slightly. Maria held her breath for a moment.

They heard the same thing—but interpreted it differently. And yet, there was a strange feeling of reflection in the air. As if they each, without knowing it, began to see their own story as part of a larger narrative.

The speaker took a sip of water and let her gaze sweep across the room.

"I'm going to ask you to do something a little unusual," she said. "You'll now have a moment to write down one word. One word that describes what you long for in your financial life. Nothing technical. Something human. A word that comes from your gut."

The room fell silent. Not an uncomfortable silence, but a close and collective calm. As if something had started to settle.

Jonas stared at his notebook for a long time. His first impulse was to write *freedom*, but something inside him resisted. He had used that word so many times before—without really knowing what it meant. His hand instead began to form another word. One that surprised him: *dignity*. He stared at it as if it had written itself. A strange warmth spread through his chest. It was as if that word was what he had been missing in all his budgets.

Maria sat with her pen over the paper. Her thoughts circled around the words balance, lightness, trust. But what she wrote was: *rhythm*. A small, unpretentious word—but with deep resonance. She didn't quite know why, but it felt right. As if her finances didn't need to be a project. Maybe more like a movement. Something alive.

They didn't see each other. They had no idea they had reached out in the same direction—just with different words. But in that moment, both sat a little straighter. As if something had begun to make sense. Not as a solution. But as a direction.

"Thank you," the speaker said softly, sensing that most had written down their word. "You've just done something important. You've listened inward. And that's rarely the first step we're encouraged to take when it comes to money."

Economic Ecology

A new slide faded onto the screen: a soft illustration of a tree with deep roots, lively branches, and small interwoven cycles between birds, leaves, fungi, and underground connections.

"Imagine your finances as part of an ecosystem," the speaker said. "Not as an isolated account, but as something that lives, grows, and reacts to its surroundings. Your choices, your rhythms, your way of using and giving money—it doesn't just affect you. It affects the whole system around you. Family. Society. Nature. The future."

Maria leaned in slightly. It was a language she knew from other contexts—environment, sustainability, relationships. But she had never thought of money that way. As something that could participate in a rhythm, rather than something that needed fixing or optimizing.

Jonas looked up at the image of the tree. It reminded him of something he had once read about mycelium—the fungal network underground where organisms communicate in secret. He had been fascinated that something so invisible could be so crucial. Maybe money was like that too. Not just what you see on the surface—but something that connects things behind the scenes.

"We rarely talk about it," the speaker continued, "but financial choices are also emotional choices. Values. Trust. Fear. Generosity. All tangled together. And the more we understand our place in it all, the more freedom we have—not to control everything, but to make conscious choices."

She let another pause fall over the room. Not for effect, but to let the participants reflect.

"So ask yourself," she concluded gently, "what role do you want to play in your own financial ecosystem?"

Jonas stayed seated and looked at the image of the tree for a long time, even after the slide had changed. Something in his chest felt loosened—as if a knot was slowly coming undone. Not because he had figured out his finances. But because it suddenly seemed possible that money wasn't just a struggle. Maybe it was also a language. A relationship. A way of living.

He thought of his mother. How she had always struggled to make ends meet. And how he himself had swung between control and chaos in his finances ever since. Maybe it wasn't just bad habits. Maybe he had inherited a way of understanding money. A way he could now choose to view with a little more kindness. A little more curiosity. Maybe even with dignity.

Further down the row, Maria sat with her eyes closed and her hand resting on her notebook. She thought about her own rhythm. How she had tried to fit into a financial narrative that didn't quite belong to her. The men she had dated. The jobs she had taken. The way she had cut back, calculated, saved, and stored. All in the hope of being responsible. But maybe also out of fear of not having enough.

She opened her eyes and wrote a small sentence beneath the word rhythm: "Maybe I don't need to save myself away, but learn to dance along."

Their eyes didn't meet. But both sat with a sense that something had changed. Not dramatically. But like an opening. A gentle movement away from self-blame and toward something more alive. An invitation to be human—even in one's finances.

Money in Circulation — Not as a Holding

"Imagine," said the speaker, "that money wasn't something you owned—but something you passed through."

She let the words hang in the air while pointing to the new image on the screen. It didn't show piles of coins or stacks of bills, but a cycle—like a bloodstream—where money moved in circles between hands, places, and purposes.

"We're used to thinking of money as holdings. Something you have—or don't have. Something you collect, save, and hold on to. But that idea often makes us forget that at its core, economics is about movement. About what we use. What we give. What we set in motion."

She walked calmly in front of the screen and continued:

"Just like blood only serves a purpose when it flows, money works best when it circulates. That doesn't mean we can't save—but we should ask ourselves: What exactly are we trying to secure? Is it future freedom? Or a shield against fear?"

Jonas shifted slightly in his seat. The words struck something he had struggled to articulate. He had always felt most secure when there was money in the account—as a shield against something undefinable. But maybe he had forgotten to ask himself what the money was actually for. And when enough was enough.

The speaker continued:

"When we see money as something that must move, we also begin to see ourselves as participants in a larger system. Every time we buy something, we support something. Every time we choose, we also choose not to. Every dollar tells a story and affects the cycle."

Maria looked down at her hands. She thought about the small decisions she had made over the past week. Which store she had chosen. What she had decided not to buy because it seemed too expensive. What she had passed on. It was as if her financial story suddenly had chapters she hadn't noticed before.

The Hidden Influence — How Our Financial Choices Spread

"Most of us think our financial choices are private," said the speaker with a small smile. "But in reality… they trickle."

A soft laugh spread through the room. She let the pause linger for a moment before continuing:

"They trickle down into our relationships, our neighborhoods, out into society. We inspire each other, copy each other—and in some cases pressure each other. Financial behavior is rarely isolated."

A new image appeared on the screen: a row of silhouettes connected by lines—like a network. Next to each person were small icons: a coffee cup, a bicycle, a credit card, a home, a phone. The speaker pointed to the figure in the middle.

"Imagine this person—let's call her Anna. Anna just bought a new phone. Not because she needed one, but because her coworkers started talking about the new features. And now Anna's friend, who had planned to wait another year, starts thinking maybe it's time to upgrade after all."

She turned to the audience: "Is that consumer pressure? Maybe. But it's also a form of social resonance. Money is contagious."

Jonas leaned forward slightly. It reminded him of the time one of his friends started renovating his house. Not long after, Jonas himself had requested quotes for new windows—without really knowing why.

Maria nodded to herself. She thought about the times when her friends' choices made her feel wrong. As if she should want the same, buy the same, live the same way. And how it had felt like a relief the few times someone said: "I skipped it—I just didn't feel like it."

The speaker continued:

"We don't have to be victims of it. We can choose to be aware of how we influence—and are influenced. Financial awareness isn't just about knowing your budget. It's about knowing your place in a network. Who sees you? And who do you mirror yourself in?"

She let her gaze slowly drift across the rows.

"That's why financial change rarely starts in the bank. It starts in conversations. In small choices. In the realization that your money isn't only yours."

Micro and Macro — The Value of Everyday Awareness

The speaker took a breath as if to shift gears.

"We often talk about big changes," she said. "Political decisions, sustainable investments, system shifts. But what we often forget is that the biggest changes almost always start small."

She changed the slide. On the screen appeared an image of a woman sitting in a café with a cloth bag in her lap and a reusable cup in front of her.

"This isn't an ad," she said. "It's a daily movement."

A gentle laugh rippled through the room, but the atmosphere was attentive.

"Conscious economics begins with everyday choices. Which store we shop at. How we use what we already own. Who we support when we click, share, or recommend something."

She leaned in slightly, her eyes seeking connection.

"You might think it doesn't make a difference. But if you ask someone who depends on local customers, they'll tell you it does. It matters whether you buy your coffee here or there. It matters whether you recommend the small independent shop—or only engage with those who can afford to dominate your algorithm."

Jonas nodded almost imperceptibly. He had tried to shop locally himself, but sometimes he hadn't had the energy to follow through on his intentions. Now it seemed like it might be more important than he'd thought.

Maria felt a warmth spreading in her chest. She thought of the small clothing shop in her neighborhood where the owner always greeted her by name. She had almost forgotten how much it meant to be seen—even as a customer. And maybe right there: as a human being.

Finances as Rhythm — A Shared Responsibility

"But it's not just about conscious choices," the speaker continued. "It's also about rhythm."

The screen changed to an image of the tides. An ocean that recedes and returns again and again—calm, regular, alive.

"Our finances needs to breathe," she said. "It doesn't always have to be growing. It needs pauses, setbacks, regeneration. Just like us. Finances isn't a machine. It's an organism."

She paused. Not heavily, but like a quiet inhale.

"And we're all part of that organism. We create the rhythm with our choices—with our ways of giving and taking, spending and resting, saving and letting go."

Maria watched the undulating movement on the screen and thought about her own rhythm. How she often either held too tightly or let go too much. How it rarely felt balanced—more like all-or-nothing than like a cycle.

The speaker smiled gently.

"There's no one right rhythm," she said. "But there are balances you can learn to feel. And it starts by asking: What does my own financial cycle really look like? Where in my life does the money flow? Where does it stop? And what am I really trying to hold onto—or avoid?"

She let her gaze move calmly over the audience.

"It's not just your responsibility," she added. "It's all of ours. Because when we talk about money, we're really talking about life. And how we choose to live it—together."

Money as a Cycle — Giving and Receiving in Balance

It began as an almost imperceptible shift in the room's atmosphere. The speaker's voice softened, and her pace slowed slightly. She looked around as if she wanted to capture everyone's attention on a deeper level.

"We've talked about money as value, as security, as choice," she said. "But tonight, I want to invite you to think of money as something that flows."

On the screen behind her, an image appeared of a river gently winding through a landscape.

"Everything in nature moves in cycles," she continued. "The seasons. The moon phases. Sleep and wakefulness. Inhaling and exhaling. Even the earth rests between harvests. But we've grown up with an economic ideal that almost exclusively focuses on accumulation, control, and optimization. We hold on. We protect. We fear loss."

She let the silence settle for a moment. Then added, with warmth in her voice:

"There is another way. A more feminine approach to economics. An economic ecology, you might call it. It doesn't see money as something to grip tightly—but as something that should move in rhythm—with us, with others, with life."

The room grew quiet. Not out of politeness, but because the words had landed somewhere they could take root.

"This approach isn't about gender," she said. "But about quality. It's a way of being in economics where intuition, timing, care, and trust have room to participate. Where we dare both to give and to receive. Where we understand that when we hold on too tightly, we create blockages. And when we open up, something begins to flow again—also within ourselves."

Theoretical Perspectives — When Money Moves with Meaning

"It might sound poetic," the speaker said with a crooked smile, "but there are actually strong theories and experiences behind this approach to money as movement and rhythm."

She changed the image. On the screen was a woman standing with her arms outstretched in nature, the wind in her hair.

"Vicky Robin," she said, "an American economic thinker, has written about money as life energy. Every time we spend money, we're really spending a piece of our time, our attention, our life force. She suggests we begin to ask ourselves: Does this actually make sense in relation to my life? Does it feel like a fair trade for my life energy?"

There were nods around the room—slow, thoughtful.

"Another important thinker, Amartya Sen, economist and Nobel laureate, doesn't just talk about income and consumption. He talks about *capabilities*—our actual ability to act. Economics isn't just about having, but about being able. What matters isn't the amount of money, but our ability to convert it into action, into choices, into life."

She paused briefly. Let the sentences resonate. Then changed tone.

"And then there's Kate Northrup," she said with a sparkle in her voice. "She talks about the *feminine finances*—a way of engaging with money that follows your own rhythms. She works with cycles, with pauses, and with the timing of the body and nature. Not as an opposition to strategy or structure—but as an alternative to constant pressure and linear growth. She asks: What happens when we also make room for rest, for introspection, for doing nothing—and not only for doing and achieving?"

She looked up, letting her gaze rest quietly on the audience.

"These aren't just theories," she said softly. "They're invitations. Invitations to let economics begin to move as something more organic. Something that isn't separate from us—but in sync with us. And maybe—if we dare—with each other."

When Money Gets Blocked — and When It Flows

The speaker let her gaze calmly sweep across the room.

"Imagine," she said, "a woman who has been saving for years. She has a considerable amount in her account, but every time she considers spending a little—on herself, on a course, on a trip—something tightens in her body. She feels discomfort. Her shoulders tense. She thinks: 'Maybe there's a bill I haven't foreseen. Maybe I should wait.' And then nothing happens. The money stands still. But so does she. There is no movement."

She let the words settle. They glided silently into the room and stuck.

"Or imagine a man who always spends money as soon as it comes in. Not because he's necessarily irresponsible—but because it's his way of creating a sense of control, of pleasure, of feeling alive. But at the same time, it creates a spiral where he never truly feels free. Because he's always chasing the next opportunity, the next purchase, the next relief. Here, the money flows—but without rhythm. It doesn't become a cycle. It becomes a leak."

She let the silence hang for a moment before continuing—gently, almost intimately:

"But then there are those where something begins to flow—in a different way. A woman chooses to support her friend's project. Not because she expects a return, but because it feels right. A man gives money to his nephew—with no conditions—and experiences a sense of freedom in it. A family decides to restructure their finances so they work less and have more time. And suddenly, the money that once felt scarce now actually feels like enough."

She smiled—softly, sincerely.

"Money can block us. It can freeze. But it can also loosen something, set things in motion, create connections. It all depends on whether we dare give it space to move. And whether we dare ask ourselves: Is this a movement I want to be part of?"

Money as Social Rhythm — and Rhythm Disruptions

"We often think money is something private," the speaker said, as a new slide faded in— a simple cycle with arrows between people. "But money is always social. Even when we spend it alone, it happens within a network of expectations, norms, reflections, and agreements. Money isn't just a resource—it's also a rhythm we move in, together."

She let the words linger for a moment before continuing:

"Think about how a dinner gets canceled when someone says: 'I can't afford it.' Or how awkward it can feel to offer to pay for someone—as if it triggers something unspoken. Or how we sometimes avoid telling others we got a raise, because it might create imbalance. All these situations show us that money isn't just numbers. It's also relationships."

She paused briefly and took a deep breath.

"When the rhythm is disrupted—when we're afraid to talk about money in our relationships, when gift-giving turns into guilt, when we hide our spending from those closest to us—the rhythm becomes staccato. Uneven. We lose connection. But the good news is: The rhythm can be restored. Through openness. By daring to share what feels vulnerable. By creating spaces where money isn't taboo—but a shared project."

Now a quote appeared on the slide in simple lettering:

"Rhythm arises when something is given—and something is received."

"It might sound simple," said the speaker, "but it's actually revolutionary. We've grown up in a society where money is about performance and control. But what if it could also be about connection, about balance, about reciprocity?"

Finding One's Place in the Whole

After a brief pause, the speaker rose slightly from her chair, looked out over the participants, and began the conclusion of her talk.

"Many people think that money is about one of two things: Either making ends meet—or optimizing and investing. But today I'd like to leave you with another thought:

Financial responsibility is not just a civic duty. It's a life duty. An opportunity. A path to step into character—not just as a consumer or taxpayer, but as a human being."

She now spoke more slowly. Each sentence carried its own weight.

"When we begin to understand how money moves in our lives—how we receive it, use it, and what we're really longing for through it—then we also begin to understand ourselves.

It's a path of personal development.

Not necessarily to save the world—though that might happen too—but to find one's own place. In daily life. In society. In the world."

She paused briefly, as if letting it settle within the participants.

"It takes courage to look at your own pattern. To examine what you avoid. What you repeat. Where you close your eyes. But only then can you begin to choose yourself.

And that's why: Economic ecology is not just about sustainability out there. It's about becoming aware—inside. And from there, stepping into a movement where you don't just consume—but contribute.

With awareness. With choice. With integrity."

When the Rhythm Is Felt on the Way Home

After the talk ended, a calm settled over the room—one no one seemed eager to break. Jonas stood up slowly, pushed his chair back in place, and cast one last glance at the stage, where the speaker was gathering her papers. He hadn't said a word the entire session—just listened. Listened to something that, in a strange way, had resonated.

Without fully knowing why, he decided not to take the bus right away. Instead, he started walking—through the city streets, past parked cars and dark shop windows. He felt his thoughts begin to flow, like water under the skin:

What if money isn't just about what I have—but about how I move… and how I let something flow.

When he got home and dropped his keys in the bowl by the door, he didn't turn on the light right away. He stood still for a moment in the dark. Listened to the silence. Thought about the transfer to his mother he had postponed for so long. Not because he didn't have the money. But because…

…it felt vulnerable. To be someone who owes. To receive.

But maybe—maybe that too was a way of being in rhythm.

At nearly the same time, Maria got on her bike. She coasted home against a light headwind, smiling without quite knowing why. Something in the lecture had stuck. Something about money as rhythm. Something about how we are always in relationship—even when we think we act alone.

When she got home, she put on a kettle and logged into her online bank. A message from her cousin was waiting: She had started a small ceramics studio and asked if Maria could support the project with a contribution.

Maria quickly typed in $40 and sent it off—spontaneously, without much thought.

Only afterward, while clearing the kitchen table, did she feel it. That warm sensation. Not because she had given something away, but because she had shared. Something was in motion.

'Money as rhythm,' she thought. 'It actually feels… alive.'

Exercise: Your Finances as a Living Cycle

Imagine your finances as water in nature. It flows through your life like rain, rivers, lakes, and evaporation—bringing nourishment, movement, and rhythm.

This exercise invites you to draw and reflect—not as an artist, but as an explorer. It's not about aesthetics, but about insight.

Draw your financial cycle like a water cycle

Start by drawing a simple natural scene. It can be naïve and personal:

- A cloud
- A mountain
- A river
- A lake
- A tree with roots and branches
- The sun warming and causing evaporation

Add symbols to your drawing

Now connect the movement of water to your finances:

- The cloud represents the origin of your money—salary, pension, gifts, support
- The rain represents receiving—how you feel when money comes in
- The river is the movement of money through your life—your expenses and actions
- The lake is your savings—or the place you seek financial calm
- The tree is your values—what you nourish and want to grow
- The sun and evaporation are the hidden flows—unconscious patterns, spontaneous purchases, old habits

Reflect with small questions at each symbol

Write just a few words around your drawing:

- By the cloud: Where does my money come from? And how do I feel about it?
- By the rain: How do I receive money? With joy? Worry? Guilt?
- By the river: How does money flow in my life? Steady? Turbulent? Does it leak away?
- By the lake: Do I feel secure? Do I experience drought or flooding?
- By the tree: What do I want to nourish? Which branches should grow in my life?
- By the sun: Is there something hidden I need to notice?

Conclusion — Your Economic Ecosystem

Now look at your drawing and ask yourself:

- Where in my cycle do I most need to shift the rhythm?

- What would I like to nourish—and where might I let go of some control?

You don't need to have clear answers to everything. Maybe it's enough just to see it with new eyes. Maybe that's where the movement begins.

Resonance — Standing in Your Financial Landscape

When the lights dim and the talk is over, some people remain seated for a while. Not because they're waiting for more—but because something is already in motion. A look inward. A kind of resonance.

Maybe, as a reader, you've felt the same along the way.

Maybe you've discovered that money isn't just about calculating—but also about feeling. That money isn't just numbers, but also moods. Stories. Dreams. Hidden shame rooms. And untapped possibilities.

We've talked about domains and agendas. About psychology and behavior patterns. About budgets, shadows, and gift economies. We've seen how even small decisions contain big stories—and how knowing your financial style is also about knowing yourself.

But most importantly:

We've pointed to a movement.

A movement toward stepping into character. Not as a financial expert—but as a human being in your own life.

To take your place in the economic ecosystem doesn't necessarily mean doing something grand, but doing something honest. It means daring to stay awake. To face your choices. And maybe—to begin choosing with your heart.

Because it's in the meeting between the outer and the inner, between values and habits, that financial responsibility becomes human freedom.

And that's where something new begins.

A Look Back — and Ahead

What You've Been Through — and What You Can Take with You

Maybe it doesn't feel like you've read a book about money. Maybe it felt more like a conversation. Or a journey through layers you may have known—but never put into words before.

This book hasn't given you a recipe. Instead, it tried to give you a mirror. And an inner route you can now see more clearly.

Here's an overview of the key psychological steps you've taken along the way:

From Control to Curiosity

You started with a feeling: That money takes up more space than it should—but in a way that isn't just about numbers.

You saw how financial control often hides emotional insecurity, and how spreadsheets and ideals can feel like judges if they don't account for who you are.

From Self-Criticism to Self-Understanding

You discovered that many financial decisions aren't wrong—they're just unconscious.

When we look honestly at our finances, we don't just see spending. We see values, longings, wounds, and strengths. It's not about behaving correctly—but about understanding why we do what we do.

From Shame to Integrity

Along the way, you may have met parts of yourself you usually avoid: impulses, repetitions, evasions.

But you also met the possibility of seeing them with kindness—not as weaknesses, but as traces telling a story.

When you understand your financial shadows, you can begin to take responsibility—not as a burden, but as a way to be honest with yourself.

From Scarcity to Possibility

You've encountered concepts like mental accounting, domain thinking, and behavioral economics—not as theories, but as keys to understanding your reality.

You may have discovered that you already have more resources than you thought—and that the feeling of wealth begins with how you view what you already have.

From Loneliness to Humanity

Maybe you've felt a little less alone.

In the stories of Maria and Jonas, and in the questions you've reflected on yourself, you've met a community—not of perfect economists, but of people trying to align their lives and their money.

And now?

Now something new begins. Not because you're finished. But because you've found a new starting point.

A financial life that begins from within.

A life where money isn't just something you have—but something you choose to use with meaning.

A life where financial responsibility isn't about following others' models—but about taking your own values seriously.

You don't need to be perfect. You don't need to have all the answers.

But you can start asking the right questions. And that's already a step.

A Personal Afterword

I've personally struggled for a long time to find the right place for money in my life. Not just to make the numbers add up—but to find a way to be in the world where money doesn't trip me up, but becomes a natural and meaningful part of who I am.

I wanted to be able to look myself in the mirror—even when talking about money. I wanted to make financial choices that aligned with my values and worldview. And that took time.

An important key along the way has been the idea of a mental finances—or, as I also call it: an ecological finances. A language that made it possible for me to think in more nuanced terms. Not in rows and columns, but in life.

Here, the theory of domains helped me. It taught me that money isn't just money. That money can strengthen—or weaken—parts of my personality. And that my desire to become more whole, more real, more myself... couldn't be separated from money. It had to come along.

It's my hope that this book has given you something. A language. An opening. A rhythm.

Maybe you now feel that there is another way to talk about money. Not just the bank's, not just the global finances's. But also a more sensory, rhythmic, perhaps even more feminine way. A way where you can find your own place—in life, in the everyday, in the finances.

Thank you for reading!

Appendix

THE PEOPLE BEHIND THE IDEAS

Many of the ideas you've encountered in this book don't stand alone—they're built on thoughtful research, philosophical reflections, and personal experiences. In this appendix, you'll find brief presentations of some of the theorists and writers who have inspired the book's approach.

The individuals you'll meet here come from diverse fields—economics, psychology, anthropology, philosophy. What they share is an attempt to understand how we humans relate to money, security, choices, and values—not just in theory, but in practice.

The purpose of these introductions isn't to provide exhaustive summaries, but to offer you, the reader, a quick overview:

Who are they?

What are their central ideas?

And how do they contribute to the economic self-understanding this book seeks to open up?

If one of them piques your interest, you might benefit from exploring their books, lectures, or articles. You may discover that economics doesn't have to be a foreign language—but can become a path to greater personal and human clarity.

Amartya Sen

Brief Biography

Amartya Sen (b. 1933) is an Indian economist, philosopher, and Nobel laureate, best known for his work on welfare, poverty, development economics, and social justice. He has taught at many of the world's most prestigious universities, including Harvard and Cambridge. In 1998, he received the Nobel Prize in Economics for his contributions to welfare theory and social choice.

Key Ideas

Amartya Sen's approach to economics differs significantly from classical utility-based thinking. Instead of measuring welfare by consumption, income, or preferences, he focuses on capabilities—what people are actually able to do and be in their lives. For Sen, economic development isn't just about growth, but about freedom and real opportunities.

A central aspect of Sen's thinking is that poverty isn't just a lack of money, but a lack of capabilities and participation in society. Economic systems should therefore be evaluated by their ability to promote human well-being and freedom.

Relevance to This Book

Sen's ideas especially inspire the chapter on economic domains, life choices, and financial security.

His concept of "real freedoms" helps the reader understand that financial security and wealth aren't necessarily about the size of one's bank account, but about the ability to live the life one wants.

He also aligns with the book's ecological and psychological approach: that financial responsibility isn't just about control and numbers, but about developing judgment, surplus, and community participation.

Further Reading

- *Development as Freedom* (1999) — A foundational text in his theory of freedom.
- *The Idea of Justice* (2009) — A philosophical challenge to classical economic justice thinking.
- Articles and lectures on poverty, choice, and the capability approach.

Mary Douglas

Brief Biography

Mary Douglas (1921—2007) was a British anthropologist known for her pioneering work at the intersection of culture, religion, and everyday life. She was a professor of social anthropology at University College London and had a major influence on anthropology, sociology, and economic thinking.

Key Ideas

Mary Douglas's best-known work is *Purity and Danger* (1966), in which she explores how cultures organize the world using concepts like purity, pollution, and taboo. She shows that what we perceive as 'dirty' or 'sacred' often relates to social order and boundaries—not to objective health or value.

She later developed theories on gifts, rituals, and household economic behavior. She demonstrated that financial choices aren't just about utility and rationality, but also about symbols, status, and social codes.

Relevance to This Book

Douglas's ideas play a key role in the chapters on gifts, inheritance, and sacred money.

She helps us understand why certain money—such as a gift from a parent, an inheritance, or a sentimental object—can't be treated as 'ordinary money.'

Her theory of 'the untouchable' and 'the importance of placement' explains why we sometimes hesitate to spend certain money—or feel particularly obligated by it.

She also opens up an understanding of how everyday financial behavior often follows cultural patterns and symbols we're not conscious of—and how greater awareness can help us act more freely and mindfully in our economic relationships.

Further Reading

- *Purity and Danger* (1966)
- *The World of Goods* (1979, with Baron Isherwood): An alternative take on consumption and values in everyday economics.
- Articles on gift exchange, rituals, and household economics.

Richard H. Thaler

Brief Biography

Richard Thaler (b. 1945) is an American behavioral economist and professor at the University of Chicago. He received the Nobel Prize in Economics in 2017 for his work integrating psychological realism into economic models, especially in decision theory. He is one of the main figures behind the concept of nudging and co-author of the bestseller "Nudge" (2008), written with legal scholar Cass Sunstein.

Key Ideas

Thaler challenges the idea that people always make rational economic decisions.

Instead, he shows how we're often driven by habits, emotions, limited attention, and social norms—and how small changes in choice architecture can help us make better decisions without taking away our freedom.

One of his best-known concepts is mental accounting, where we perceive and handle money differently depending on its origin and purpose—even though a dollar is a dollar.

Relevance to This Book

Thaler is the book's central economic theorist in the chapters on mental habits, budgeting, and financial behavior.

His concept of mental accounting is directly used to explain why we often have an unrealistic or emotional relationship with money—and how it can distort our real priorities and choices.

His work also points toward solutions where we don't necessarily need more self-control, but rather frameworks and awareness that guide us forward.

Further Reading

- *Nudge: Improving Decisions About Health, Wealth, and Happiness* (2008, with Cass Sunstein)
- *Misbehaving: The Making of Behavioral Economics* (2015): A personal and humorous account of Thaler's journey as a behavioral economist.
- Articles on mental accounting, nudging, and financial self-control found in various behavioral economics collections.

Gabor Maté

Brief Biography

Gabor Maté (b. 1944) is a Hungarian-Canadian physician, author, and speaker known for his work on trauma, addiction, stress, and mental health. He spent decades working with marginalized communities in Vancouver and has written several acclaimed books.

Key Ideas

Maté's core idea is that many of our psychological and physical challenges stem from unresolved trauma, internal tension, and suppressed emotions.

He speaks about how we adapt to our surroundings early in life by suppressing our needs—and how this adaptation can manifest in the body and mind.

For Maté, healing involves reconnecting with oneself, one's nervous system, and one's authenticity.

Relevance to This Book

Maté's voice is especially relevant in the chapters on psychological safety, inner security, and financial shadows.

His thoughts help us understand that financial insecurity often isn't just about numbers and resources, but about old wounds and feelings of powerlessness that we've learned to live with.

Maté inspires us to ask: What in my financial life isn't really about money—but about fear, shame, or old patterns? And how can I meet that with care instead of control?

Further Reading

- *When the Body Says No: The Cost of Hidden Stress* (2003)
- *In the Realm of Hungry Ghosts* (2008)
- *The Myth of Normal* (2022)

Amy Cuddy

Brief Biography

Amy Cuddy (b. 1972) is an American social psychologist, researcher, and speaker known for her work on body language, self-perception, and psychological strength. She gained international recognition for her TED Talk "Your Body Language May Shape Who You Are," one of the most viewed TED Talks ever. Cuddy has taught at Harvard Business School and authored the book Presence (2015).

Key Ideas

Cuddy's research focuses on how we can change our psychological state and self-image through bodily and mental adjustments—what she calls 'presence.'

A central idea in her work is that we don't just communicate to others through our body and attitude—we also communicate to ourselves.

She shows that small, intentional changes in posture or internal narrative can help us feel more confident, safe, and true to ourselves—especially in vulnerable situations.

Relevance to This Book

Cuddy's perspectives are particularly relevant in chapters dealing with financial self-worth, the courage to act differently, and building inner security.

Her ideas complement those of Vicky Robin and Brené Brown on authenticity and personal integrity: If we feel powerless, we can't create sustainable change—not even in our finances.

Cuddy offers concrete tools for strengthening ourselves from within, making us better equipped to make financial decisions aligned with our values and desires.

Further Reading

- *Presence: Bringing Your Boldest Self to Your Biggest Challenges* (2015)
- Interviews and articles in outlets such as Harvard Business Review on confidence, social hierarchies, and self-perception.

Daniel Kahneman

Brief Biography

Daniel Kahneman (1934—2023) was an Israeli-American psychologist and Nobel laureate in economics. He is best known for his groundbreaking work in behavioral economics, developed in collaboration with Amos Tversky. In 2002, he received the Nobel Prize for showing how human decision-making often deviates from rational expectations.

Key Ideas

Kahneman's theory explores how people think and make decisions—often without realizing it. In his book Thinking, Fast and Slow (2011), he describes two systems of thinking:

System 1: fast, intuitive, emotionally driven.

System 2: slow, analytical, conscious.

Kahneman shows that we use System 1 most of the time—often at the expense of more reflective decisions. We're influenced by cognitive biases such as status quo bias, loss aversion, and confirmation bias, which lead us to repeat patterns, fear losses more than we value gains, and see what we want to see.

Relevance to This Book

Kahneman's research is central to understanding why we often act financially 'illogically'—even when we're trying to do the right thing. His ideas are especially relevant in chapters on financial behavior, the feeling of security, and unconscious patterns.

His work helps us understand why self-awareness and conscious reflection are essential if we want to change our financial habits and become more true to ourselves. He supports the book's aim to approach money as a psychological process—not just accounting.

Further Reading

- *Thinking, Fast and Slow* (2011)
- Interviews and conversations with Richard Thaler, Cass Sunstein, and Michael Lewis.

Morgan Housel

Brief Biography

Morgan Housel is an American financial writer, former columnist for The Wall Street Journal, and a partner at Collaborative Fund, an investment firm focused on future trends and behavioral economics. He is best known for his book The Psychology of Money (2020), which quickly became a bestseller and made him one of the most widely read economic communicators of recent times.

Key Ideas

Housel's core message is that financial success is more about behavior and psychology than mathematical skills. He shows how emotions, experiences, habits, and personal stories guide our financial decisions—often without us realizing it.

He emphasizes that money isn't just a matter of rational choices but also about patience, expectations, fear, and hope. Housel discusses the idea of 'enough'—knowing when we have enough and how the pursuit of more can become destructive if we don't understand why we want it.

Relevance to This Book

Housel's approach is important in this book's effort to link money to human behavior and life choices.

His thoughts help us ask: What is enough for me? What do money really mean to me—and why? He inspires an honest conversation with oneself and shows that financial responsibility doesn't have to be perfect—it just needs to match one's life and values.

Further Reading

- *The Psychology of Money* (2020): 19 short essays on money and human behavior.
- *Same As Ever* (2023): Reflections on why some things never change—and what that means for our understanding of the future and financial decisions.
- Articles and essays on morganhousel.com—often with philosophical and psychological perspectives on money.

Brené Brown

Brief Biography

Brené Brown is an American researcher, professor, and author specializing in social work and emotional psychology. She gained international fame after her TED Talk "The Power of Vulnerability," which is one of the most viewed TED Talks ever. Her research focuses on vulnerability, courage, shame, and empathy—and how these concepts are closely tied to authentic living and relationships.

Key Ideas

Brené Brown's core message is that vulnerability is not a weakness, but a prerequisite for genuine connection and courageous action. She shows how we often try to control or hide our feelings of inadequacy and shame—which can make us emotionally closed off and distant.

Through concepts like wholehearted living and shame resilience, she encourages us to show up as we are—even when we feel insecure, inadequate, or afraid.

Relevance to This Book

Brown's insights are woven throughout several chapters—especially those that explore how money, status, and finances can deeply affect our sense of self.

Her research helps us understand why money can be taboo, and why it often feels vulnerable to talk openly about financial choices, concerns, or dreams—especially in romantic relationships, families, and communities.

Her perspective also opens the door to a more empathetic and honest relationship with money—both toward ourselves and others. It makes space for the human side of economics and reminds us that financial responsibility also involves being brave in our lives.

Further Reading

- *Daring Greatly: How the Courage to Be Vulnerable Transforms the Way We Live, Love, Parent, and Lead*
- *The Gifts of Imperfection: Let Go of Who You Think You're Supposed to Be and Embrace Who You Are*
- *Atlas of the Heart: Mapping Meaningful Connection and the Language of Human Experience*

Vicki Robin

Brief Biography

Vicki Robin is an American author, social innovator, and speaker, best known for her groundbreaking book *Your Money or Your Life,* co-authored with Joe Dominguez. For decades, she's been a central figure in the movements for simple living, sustainability, and financial independence. Her economic thinking is shaped by life experience, social critique, and the desire to live in deeper harmony with her values and environment.

Key Ideas

Robin's philosophy centers around the idea that money isn't just a medium of exchange, but a representation of our life energy. Every time we spend money, we also spend the time and life it took to earn it.

She calls for a more conscious and values-based approach to money, where we ask: Does this expense truly enhance my life quality?

A key element in her method is daily awareness of spending—not as control, but as clarity. She introduces concepts like 'life energy,' 'true needs,' and 'the enough point'—where more money or things no longer increase life quality.

Relevance to This Book

Robin's ideas serve as a backbone for this book. Her notion of economic domain thinking—that money doesn't have one value but many functions depending on the life area—is central to our approach.

Her focus on money being in service of the life we want to live, rather than the other way around, underlies many of the reflections, exercises, and examples in the book.

Robin also inspired the tone of this book: a warm and curious approach to money, inviting the reader to find their own language and balance.

Further Reading

- Interviews and talks on YouTube, particularly in FIRE and simplicity circles
- Articles on vickirobin.com, where she shares new insights and conversations about life, finances, and society

Kate Northrup

Brief Biography

Kate Northrup is an American author and entrepreneur, known for her books Money: A Love Story and Do Less. Her work operates at the intersection of finance, femininity, rhythm, motherhood, and personal awareness. She has helped pave the way for an economic perspective rooted not in growth and achievement, but in vitality, balance, and trust in one's own rhythms.

Relevance to This Book

Kate Northrup represents one of the clearest voices for what might be called a feminine approach to finance. She encourages us to feel ourselves before we measure ourselves. While many financial books focus on structure, planning, and external control, Northrup's universe is about cycles, intuition, and inner trust.

In this book, her perspective inspired us to see financial responsibility not as a project, but as a rhythm. Not as a spreadsheet, but as a movement. Her ideas helped us find language for how to be financially conscious without being self-controlling—and how to care for our money without compromising our humanity.

Challenging Constant Achievement

A central aspect of Northrup's philosophy is that more isn't always better. She writes especially for women who've tried to live up to ideals of constant productivity and financial perfectionism—and who are exhausted by it. Her ideas about 'do less to achieve more' point instead toward finding a financial flow that is sustainable, gentle, and deeply satisfying.

Further Reading

- *Money: A Love Story — Untangle Your Financial Woes and Create the Life You Really Want* (2013)
- *Do Less — A Revolutionary Approach to Time and Energy Management for Ambitious Women* (2019)
- Podcast: *The Kate & Mike Show*
- Digital resources and courses at katenorthrup.com

Sigmund Freud

Brief Biography

Sigmund Freud (1856–1939) was an Austrian neurologist and the founder of psychoanalysis—a revolutionary approach to understanding the human mind that continues to influence psychology, philosophy, art, and culture to this day. Freud was born in what was then the Austro-Hungarian Empire (now the Czech Republic) and spent most of his professional life in Vienna. His theories have been both passionately embraced and sharply criticized, but his impact on modern self-understanding is undeniable. He died in exile in London in 1939.

Core Ideas

Freud envisioned the human psyche as composed of three constantly conflicting parts:

- *The id – the unconscious,* instinct-driven part of us that seeks pleasure and immediate gratification.
- *The ego – the conscious self,* which tries to mediate between external demands and internal urges.
- *The superego – the internalized conscience and moral authority,* carrying norms, rules, and ideals, often inherited from parents and society.

This dynamic model explains much of our behavior, Freud argued, as the result of inner conflict between what we desire, what we believe we should do, and what we actually do. He believed that a great deal of our behavior—including irrational decisions—stems from unconscious drives and repressed emotions.

Relevance for This Book

In this book, we explore personal finance as a psychological and existential landscape—and Freud's model of personality offers powerful tools for this exploration.

For example, when we make an impulsive purchase we can't afford, it may be the id that's in charge, driven by desire and immediate need. When we later feel ashamed or self-critical, it's often the superego stepping in with judgment. And in between stands the ego, trying to make it all work—rationally, but often under pressure.

This inner economic triangle is highly relevant when examining spending habits, debt, consumerism, and self-image. Financial choices are rarely just about numbers and spreadsheets—they are often about internal negotiations between longing, shame, and responsibility. By becoming aware of these dynamics, we can approach our financial life with more honesty and freedom.

Freud's concepts give us a language for inner economic conflict—and help us uncover what parts of ourselves we may (unconsciously) be trying to satisfy, hide, or live up to when we spend money.

Further Reading

For those who wish to explore Freud's theories and their relevance today, the following are recommended:

- *The Ego and the Id* (1923) – Freud's foundational text introducing the id, ego, and superego model.
- *An Outline of Psychoanalysis* (posthumously published, 1940) – A concise overview of his later thinking.
- Peter Gay: Freud: *A Life for Our Time* – A nuanced and widely respected biography.
- For a modern psychological interpretation: Jonathan Shedler (articles and lectures), who revives Freud's insights in contemporary psychotherapy.

Barry Schwartz

Brief Biography

Barry Schwartz (b. 1946) is an American psychologist and Professor Emeritus at Swarthmore College, where he taught psychology for several decades. His work lies at the intersection of psychology, ethics, society, and everyday life—with a particular focus on how modern choices and living conditions affect our mental well-being and overall quality of life. Schwartz is known as a compelling communicator and has delivered several popular TED Talks. He is the author of numerous books, including the internationally acclaimed *The Paradox of Choice.*

Core Ideas

In The Paradox of Choice (2004), Schwartz presents a simple yet profound idea: more options don't necessarily make us happier—in fact, they can leave us more dissatisfied, more anxious, and more paralyzed.

In an era defined by endless opportunities and constant information overload, Schwartz shows how we are often overwhelmed by choice rather than delighted by it. He distinguishes between two types of people:

- *Maximizers*—those who strive to find the absolute best option, meticulously exploring all possibilities. They often end up exhausted and discontented.
- *Satisficers*—those who are content with a "good enough" choice. They are generally more satisfied and less stressed.

Schwartz argues that the more choices we have, the more likely we are to regret the one we made. Additionally, our expectations rise—often to unrealistic levels—which can leave us disappointed even when we've made a perfectly good choice.

Relevance for This Book

In this book, we explore personal finance as something deeply human and emotionally charged. Schwartz's theory provides sharp insight into modern consumer culture: when we constantly believe there's something better "out there," we tend to chase quantity instead of enjoying quality. We compare ourselves to others, obsess over missed opportunities, and doubt whether we chose correctly.

His concept of the tyranny of choice sheds light on the inner unrest many people experience when making financial decisions—both big and small. Rather than seeking the perfect outcome, we might take inspiration from Schwartz and practice being satisfied with "good enough," rediscovering the peace and joy in the choices we've already made.

Further Reading

If you'd like to delve deeper into Barry Schwartz's thinking, consider the following:

- *The Paradox of Choice: Why More is Less* (2004) – His seminal work combining research, everyday psychology, and cultural insight.
- TED Talk: *The Paradox of Choice – A thought-provoking and accessible introduction* (available on TED.com or YouTube).
- *Practical Wisdom: The Right Way to Do the Right Thing* (with Kenneth Sharpe, 2010) – On how we can make wise and ethical choices in everyday life, despite uncertainty and complexity.

Søren Kierkegaard

Brief Biography

Søren Aabye Kierkegaard (1813–1855) was a Danish theologian, philosopher, and writer widely regarded as one of the founding figures of existentialism. Born into a wealthy and deeply religious family in Copenhagen, his upbringing left a lasting mark on both his life and thought. As a young man, he began writing philosophical and religious works—often under pseudonyms—and his style moved freely between philosophy, psychology, satire, and sermons. He lived a reclusive life and died relatively young, but his influence has grown immensely over time, particularly among thinkers like Heidegger, Sartre, and later psychologists and theologians.

Core Ideas

Kierkegaard's philosophy centers on the individual's relationship to self, to truth, and to God. For him, the decisive task is that each person must choose—and take responsibility for—their own existence. He introduces the concept of three stages of life:

- *The aesthetic stage*, where life is lived for pleasure and in avoidance of responsibility.
- *The ethical stage*, where the individual seeks authenticity through commitment, morality, and self-development.
- *The religious stage*, where faith and a personal relationship with God become central.

A key concept in Kierkegaard's thought is anxiety—not as a pathology, but as an existential condition. Anxiety arises when we are confronted with the freedom to choose and must do so without any guarantee of choosing rightly. Yet it is through this very choice that we become truly human—and through responsibility that we become free.

Relevance for This Book

In this book, we explore personal finances as a mirror of human life—not just in numbers, but as expressions of values, desires, and decisions. This is where Kierkegaard's ideas become especially relevant. His insistence on conscious choice—and on the idea that we become ourselves through commitment and authenticity—offers a philosophical framework for understanding why it matters whether we choose quality or quantity.

When we begin to question our financial habits and goals, the issue becomes existential: Am I living a life I've chosen—or merely the life handed to me? Kierkegaard helps us see that genuine quality of life emerges through conscious choice—and the courage to stand by it.

Further Reading

If you wish to explore Kierkegaard's thinking without getting lost in theology or dense philosophy, the following are good starting points:

- *Either/Or* (1843) – Kierkegaard's classic work on the stages of life and the contrast between the aesthetic and ethical.
- *The Concept of Anxiety* (1844) – On anxiety as an existential possibility.
- *The Sickness Unto Death* (1849) – A deeply psychological work about despair and the self.
- *To Choose Oneself* (excerpts and commentary, edited by Johannes Sløk) – A modern introduction to Kierkegaard's thoughts on choice and authenticity.

www.ingramcontent.com/pod-product-compliance
Lightning Source LLC
LaVergne TN
LVHW100308210926
848480LV00003B/1053
9798232548865